On Her, Majesty's Service

On Her, Majesty's Service

My Incredible Life in the World's Most Dangerous Close Protection Squad

RON EVANS

WITH DOUGLAS THOMPSON

JOHN BLAKE

Published by John Blake Publishing Ltd,
3 Bramber Court, 2 Bramber Road,
London W14 9PB, UK

www.blake.co.uk

First published in the United Kingdom in 2008

ISBN: 978-1-84454-602-2

British Library Cataloguing-in-Publication Data:
A catalogue record for this book is available from the British Library.

Design by www.envydesign.co.uk

Printed in the UK by CPI William Clowes
Beccles NR34 7TL

1 3 5 7 9 10 8 6 4 2

Papers used by John Blake Publishing are natural, recyclable
products made from wood grown in sustainable forests.
The manufacturing processes conform to the environmental
regulations of the country of origin.

In memory of Mum and Dad, Ron and Ella, who stood by me over the years, and for my two sons, James and Alex.

'I want you to remember that no bastard ever won a war by dying for his country. He won it by making the other poor dumb bastard die for his country.'
George C Scott as General George S Patton in *Patton* (1970)

'It's sometimes said that the only lesson that history teaches us is that no one learns from history.'
Leonard J Burt, Commander of the Special Branch (1946–58)

Acknowledgements

This book has given me the time to reflect on so many incidents and people from all walks of life, from the highest in the land to those who are not so fortunate. All of them have a place in my life. I have revealed many of the situations that I was involved in over the years yet there were some that, for operational reasons, I can never disclose.

I could not have told my story without the help of the perceptive Douglas Thompson, who skilfully guided me throughout the process. Over the months we formed a friendship and, more importantly, a trust in each other to make this all possible.

I also deeply appreciate the tenacity and professionalism of Stuart Robertson at John Blake Publishing for helping smooth the sometimes rocky path to publication.

I must give thanks to the people who have supported me and encouraged me to tell my story. To Cindy, who kept me going when I was unsure of where I was heading, and because of this she will have a special place in my heart and thoughts. To Anne who put up with the days and weeks of my being away when I put my career in front of my family and paid the price.

To Mike and Kim, Dave and Sharon, whom I have known from the early days patrolling the mean streets of southeast London in Traffic Division, and who have remained good and loyal friends. And to all those who have been in my life, some for a season, and some for a reason, I thank you all.

To all my family scattered over the country, Scotland, Yorkshire and in London and those in Croydon who behind the scenes wished me well. Not forgetting my two brothers, Peter and Paul. I'm so glad that I wasn't born a girl: it would have been too much to be called Mary. They too have given me unwavering support.

However, special thanks must go those principals (the beneficiaries of our protection duties) whom I have had, at times, the pleasure of protecting over the years. Thank you for allowing me into your lives, and treating me as a friend rather than your protection officer. I think that I did a good job; after all we didn't 'lose' anyone! Without them there wouldn't be a story to tell.

Also, to my former colleagues in A Squad, and to those officers up and down the country, and all over the world. It was a pleasure to work with you all. We had some extraordinary times and saw some tumultuous changes in the world order. A Squad had an esprit de corps that was second to none. Thank you for those times, good and bad. I wish you all good health. Remember, do it to them before they do it to you.

I have changed the names of my former colleagues, as

most of them still do dangerous and vital work for national security.

As this book was completed my mother died unexpectedly and therefore will not see the result of my endeavours. I'm filled with a sense of achievement tinged with great sadness.

I avidly read political biographies and I recall the comment of the disgraced American president Richard Nixon: 'Only someone who has been in the deepest valley knows how beautiful the tallest mountain is.'

Ron Evans, Sri Lanka, July 4th, 2008

Contents

Foreword by Douglas Thompson   xv

Introduction: BULLET CATCHER   xvii

Prologue: THE HIT SQUAD   1

Chapter 1: IN THE LINE OF FIRE   5

Chapter 2: THE KHYBER PASS   25

Chapter 3: GUN LAW   39

Chapter 4: BLOODY REVENGE   55

Chapter 5: THE SPECTRE OF DEATH   67

Chapter 6: KILLING ME SOFTLY   83

Chapter 7: HOME AFFAIRS   107

Chapter 8: BADLANDS   121

Chapter 9: THE QUEEN   145

Chapter 10: THE POLITICIAN   161

Chapter 11: COWBOYS AND CARTIER   169

Chapter 12: SECRET SERVICE   179

Chapter 13: THE BARONESS   193

Chapter 14: HELLO, SAILORS   201

Chapter 15: A FAIR COP?   209

Chapter 16: GUN SMOKE   221

Chapter 17: CHOP CHOP CITY   229

Postscript: HAVE GUN, WILL TRAVEL   237

Glossary   249

Foreword

Ron Evans is unique. He knew he would be vilified in certain quarters for writing the book you are holding. Yet he went ahead, believing he had an important story to tell.

He is the first member of the Metropolitan Police Close Protection Squad ever to tell his story and it is one that has taken nearly three years to complete. I found it a privilege working with him. The chaotic complications of his trade, and the depth of the perfidy around it, were as fascinating as they were frightening.

When the publication of On Her Majesty's Service was announced several of his former colleagues contacted me saying they also had stories to tell but thought they'd better not: there would be too much aggravation. Nevertheless they wished Ron well. Others, concerned for their own personal reasons, wrote anonymous and sometimes ominous emails about the book.

Ron Evans never wavered in his determination to tell his story – a story important to all of us today. My daughter was at King's Cross on 7/7 and thankfully survived the horror and chaos of that day while being swept up in the maelstrom of events. Friends in New York on 9/11 were not so lucky.

In our menacing modern world we never know what the next split-second might bring. Men and women like Ron Evans are walking the line, just like our troops overseas. It's important, if sometimes a terrible discomfort, to know how they work and think – and, as importantly, how they are controlled.

Prior to publication, the Metropolitan Police asked to see this book. They courteously asked for some specific but minimal changes in regards to tactical matters to protect serving and former police officers. This has willingly been done.

The Metropolitan Police also felt that the Security Service, MI5, and the Foreign Office, should also read this book before publication. This was also agreed.

This official scrutiny has not changed the narrative or tone of the story you are about to read. It enforces the importance of it.

Douglas Thompson, July 4th, 2008

Introduction
Bullet Catcher

'If you lose your man, you lose your name.'
A royal protection officer, 1988

I'm licensed to kill you.

That will happen if you appear with a weapon in your hand close to my principal, the person I'm paid to protect. Then it would be unavoidable. If I can't evade a threat it has to be eradicated. With extreme prejudice. XPD. That's my training, my skill with my Glock pistol, the seventeen-round G34 that always has one up the spout.

But it's experience, instincts and reflexes that every day I pray will continue to allow me to escape the moment when I might die for a client. I don't want to cash in from an assassination intended for someone else. Yet stepping in front of a high-velocity cartridge is part of the job, and it happens.

That's why some people call us bullet catchers.

Special Branch did not always impose the wearing of bulletproof vests, because they can restrict movement too much; instead, you use your unprotected body as a shield. Life and death maybe, but that's only part of the job. A good protection officer does just that – protects. It's better to flee with an ongoing target such as Gordon Brown or George Bush alive than turn an encounter into the Gunfight at the OK Corral.

When it's all bullets and confusion anything can happen. And anyone can get killed. It could be Lady Thatcher, whom the IRA failed to assassinate, or a world figure such as Tony Blair, who is always under threat for standing shoulder to shoulder with America and also as a peace envoy to the Middle East. He spent some years blowing Arabs up; now he wants to lead talks between them and Israel.

It's like chalking a bull's-eye around himself.

And it was prime targets such as Thatcher and Blair whom I was always invited to look after; if you're in my job, that's what gets and keeps you going, the challenge and the pumping of adrenalin.

Yet close protection is a no-win game. If your guy goes down, so does your reputation. If you pull the trigger too soon, you could face manslaughter or even murder charges.

Why do I do it? Well, it's not nine-to-five but it's my work, what I've spent a lifetime learning to do well. Staying alive, like the pension plan, is the imponderable.

I'm now employed by a private enterprise guarding diplomats and other-high profile VIPs in the Middle East and other world trouble spots. Before that, for more than twenty years, I was On Her Majesty's Service – for much of that time as a member of the Metropolitan Police Special Branch's A Squad – in what became a more and more political profession.

Then, looking after prime ministers past and present, American presidents, home secretaries, NATO officials and international manipulators of power – be they voted in or self- or God-appointed – I got an exceptional insight into how the world ticks at the top. You cannot be on life-and-death terms with these people and not acquire unique knowledge.

Today, terrorism, the threat of it, the application of it, has changed how my trade thinks and behaves. We're no longer shadows but part of the process.

I'm not sure there are or can be any mandates now. The twentieth-century rule books are obsolete; the parameters of policing violence, with the constant dread of terror, will keep changing.

Before 9/11 we knew what we were doing and who we were facing. Now that people are willing to take an express route to heaven, it's a different and increasingly terrifying story.

It's very much part of my daily life, whether I'm in the American Midwest, the Middle East or Middle England.

And, of course, a disturbing part of your life too.

Prologue
The Hit Squad

'Kill him in London.'
A diplomat is marked for death
by international drug barons

It was a nasty. The visitor was a VIP. He was marked down to die on the streets of London and the bad guys wanted the blood to flow, to make a splash of claret in city central, to make a point.

My job was to stop this high-profile assassination. The huge bastard of a problem was that the killers were ahead of the game. The hit team had discovered my guy's flight details and most of his movements in the capital.

Curdled into this was the politics – he was assessed as being a Level 1 threat. That's red hot. They really wanted him six feet under, and Her Majesty's Government couldn't have that.

On a day-to-day basis, a prime minister rates only a Level 2 alert. But for Cypriot Justice Minister Evangelos Yannopoulos it was the whole nine yards, the security works.

Which was where I came in. Even though I was posted to a

regular protection team, when emergencies happen fixers like me are invited, from time to time, to undertake other work.

That is a polite way of saying that, when the shit hits the fan, we're asked to prevent death and, as a considerable bonus, the destruction of reputations and the image of reliable and solid good ol' Blighty.

And we put our lives very much on the line. I'm not complaining. That's what keeps me alive, keeps me living.

The A Squad operation kicks off with visiting heads of state, a George Bush or a high-profile visitor such as Nelson Mandela.

The bold-headline men and women are always prime contenders for a sniper's or zealot's attention. This time around it was lethally focused. Evangelos Yannopoulos was a crusader, a politician waging war on the drug trade. The problem was that he was too successful, which had pissed off the drug barons in his own country and also traffickers in the UK. Drug merchants were either facing trial or were already in jail, which had disrupted the business of several international organisations.

The cartel's way of dealing with the problem was simple: put him in a coffin. He had XPD stamped all over him.

That coded information came from the Cypriot authorities as well as MI6 through the British High Commission. Sternly, it reported that the minister was under extreme threat and that his visit to London was going to offer the ideal opportunity for him to be killed.

As a bonus, a spy had given the killers exact details of his itinerary! When that intelligence hit London, my lot steamed into top gear. I was called into my detective chief inspector's office to 'discuss the visit of the Cypriot Justice Minister'. His death was not on the agenda; no foreign diplomat was going to die on British soil. We had our reputation.

Never mind that these high-tech, tooled-up cartel assassins were on his tail and knew his every move – those moves could not be changed, otherwise one would risk causing offence, a diplomatic hiccup.

He was coming to London to meet with the Cypriot community and to take part in a few expat festivals; he was going to be pressing the flesh, keeping the postal voters happy, and in plain sight. A target for mayhem. Meanwhile, all around, innocent civilians would be getting on buses or the Tube, walking around, shopping, without a clue that a team of killers were roaring around London and setting up their target.

Under the Vienna Convention the kindly Evangelos Yannopoulos didn't warrant protection in London. Special Branch, as an intelligence-gathering organisation, monitors countries all over the world and has a liaison officer in many. Most of the people under threat, depending on whom in the terrorist world they have upset, are assessed, as I said, at Level 2.

To give this particular visitor a Level 1 threat meant something was really going to happen – we had to be prepared. It was repeated to us enough times: there is credible information that the attack will happen, not 'likelihood', not 'possibility', but it will happen.

It wouldn't look good for the Metropolitan Police or the government to have a top foreign politician killed in the heart of London. It would similarly look bad if the government cancelled his visit. It would send out the message that Special Branch couldn't cope or didn't have the expertise to handle the situation.

We were on full alert. I checked out my Glock and 34 rounds of ammunition. Being properly armed doesn't always give you an edge against machine-gun madmen on a mission.

But it always makes me feel better.

Chapter One
In the Line
of Fire

'Remember that to change your mind and
follow him that sets you right is to be none the less
free than you were before.'
Marcus Aurelius

It felt as if a world war were about to start. The tension
of the situation – of just not knowing how big a jam we
were in – made everyone uneasy.

All intelligence said we had a dead man walking. But the
big guns were out on all sides. Literally. No expense was
spared. A full Level 1 put every sophisticated resource at
our disposal.

The team leader was DS (Detective Sergeant) Tony Patton.
I was his backup, in charge of communications and utilising
our men and weaponry as we needed. We had all manner of
police support for the armed protection team. A crucial
element of the operation was the Search Wing, the fine-
toothed-comb team, operators for whom the term 'every
nook and cranny' means just that. They can nose out
anything that just resembles a threat.

A high alert and a high stress level – perfect timing for the 'suits' to have an idea. This visit would be a good time to test all the contingency plans for a terrorist attack. And it would also be a training visit to see how other agencies co-operated with Special Branch.

I was comforted to know that we were going to be a 'live' experiment. The senior officers on the top floor always come out with startling plans at times like this!

This was a perfect example of politics and policing and, because of this, everyone had their own agenda and controller.

But the SB close-protection squad were in charge and our mission was simply to keep our distinguished visitor Evangelos Yannopoulos alive – and prevent international embarrassment.

Irrespective of rank, Tony and I had the final say in all things operational. We even outranked the Metropolitan Police commissioner if it came to it. That was the end of the matter. No arguments or need for further debate – that was written in stone and every department must comply.

The trick is to try not to use overbearing tactics. Working together, a sense that you're all pulling in the same direction, is paramount in gaining the confidence of all concerned, the belief that everyone's role is as vital as the next person's.

Protection is only as good as the weakest link and – especially this time, with such a red alert – there could be no weak links, from high command to the copper checking invitations on the door of a building being visited by our man in the line of fire.

Special Branch close-protection operations are nothing like what you see on TV or in the movies. It's far more complex and, in real life, the more low-key we can make things the better. And if you get killed you stay dead.

Yet we had to go and recce every venue and meet with

Cypriot community leaders to discuss each and every event. Nothing could be left to chance. We went to halls to check entrances and exits as well as possible vantage points from which snipers could take a shot at us.

Always, whoever the principal, the most likely point for any attack is on leaving or arriving at an event. Routes had to be checked and secondary routes to and from all venues put in place. We rejected the offer of motorcycle outriders as too overt.

We always endeavoured to be unobtrusive even with such a high threat as the Cypriot death warrant. If a target is surrounded by protection officers – we're 'bodyguards' only when it's Kevin Costner at the movies – then that person is going to feel ill at ease and uncomfortable. That feeling is twice as bad for any family that he or she may have.

That nervousness makes my job harder. It's softly-softly on the surface with a big, bad gun in your holster. And an action plan to 'lock down' all venues on our man's itinerary.

You'd be surprised at the discreet security going on all around you at times of crisis. Evangelos Yannopoulos was going to be under guard 24/7 during his very – to the British taxpayer – expensive three-day visit to London.

The Search Wing would check out and protect everywhere in London our visitor would go – and not just looking under tables, but anywhere an explosive device could be hidden, whether that be dustbins or manholes or the insides of lampposts.

Once any venue was declared 'secure', the integrity of the search would then be maintained with anyone who needed to be there escorted at all times by one of our team members.

Snipers on the roofs of nearby buildings would be used at

all locations as well as providing 24/7 cover where the minister was sleeping, which was at the Cypriot ambassador's residence in Chelsea.

At the ambassador's residence the Diplomatic Protection Group (DPG) would provide the static protection twenty-four hours a day. Armed venue protection was also their responsibility.

All the security services were in on this and because everyone wants to be lord of their manor – and everyone else's if they can pull it off – for the SB protection team it was an exercise in juggling resources and egos.

We had our own dedicated radio channel known as 'GT' direct into Scotland Yard, where information could be coordinated without adding extra pressure to the troops on the streets. GT, manned by Special Branch and high-ranking Yard officers, could also listen in to our car-to-car conversations to keep close and constant track of the operation.

In charge there was a commander – always known as 'Gold' – to make decisions in utilising the various forces involved in the alert. Yet if a decision directly involved the protection team we would have to agree with it. It's not easy to go up against such a senior officer, but I have the knowledge and expertise and he may not.

All was in place. All leave was cancelled for the next four days. Everyone was told that we would be carrying Glock handguns and fifty rounds of ammunition each. We were all ready. We went to one of the control posts at Heathrow in two bulletproof Jaguars and were escorted airside by armed airport police officers. All was going too well.

We heard through intelligence that the hit team had split up. Two were on our man's aircraft and four were already in

London. After all the planning it was 'fingers crossed' that the surveillance teams would find them. All our lives depended on it.

My reaction was that they should have been followed in Cyprus, but I was only thinking logically. Whatever the reason, we now had a major problem on our hands. It also crossed my mind that it would seem highly likely that the team in London had a safe house there, too, maybe belonging to someone we have been talking to and arranging the security with.

The connotations and consequences were not lost on any of the protection team. The information was passed back to Scotland Yard for them to deal with. We had our own problems to tend to.

The aircraft landed and, once the walkway was manoeuvred into position, we stood guard by the door. The cars, engines running, were at the bottom of the stairs waiting for the visitor to emerge.

The aircraft door swung open and the first one off was our SB desk officer Tim, who'd flown to Cyprus to 'front' the visit. Behind were the minister and his wife. Oh, good: problem times two!

As with any loyal wife, if her husband was going to be assassinated she was going to be with him. We were introduced and without further fuss escorted the group to the VIP Hounslow Suite where he was greeted by the Cypriot ambassador.

The target, in the circumstances I couldn't think of him as anything else, was slim-built and tall (6 feet), and had thick, greying hair with a moustache. He looked like Anthony Quinn in *Zorba the Greek*.

With customs and immigration formalities completed, we headed out into the unknown. Our two bulletproof Jags exited the control post gate and headed for the M4 spur road, which would lead us onto the M4 and into central London. The first stop would be the official residence of the ambassador.

As we drove onto the spur road, I looked around for any cars that might be following us. Apart from the rest of London and fears of the hit team out there, I couldn't see anyone who made me feel uncomfortable. I tried to spot our own surveillance team but because of the density of the traffic it was impossible.

Going out of the controlled airspace of Heathrow, I heard the helicopter and, looking up, saw the familiar markings of the Met chopper following our progress through the traffic. I called our control room to find out if this was a coincidence or for our benefit. I was told that the force copter would be with us for the duration of the visit.

The two cars kept close to each other. I was travelling in the backup vehicle with one of our highly trained SB drivers. His job was not to allow anything to get between us, block us, split up the team – cutting our firepower in half – and allow an attack. This called for some very aggressive driving. He liked that.

Close to the ambassador's residence the Diplomatic Protection Group radioed me the all-clear. I was not surprised: as we turned into the residence it was like a Hollywood extravaganza, a cast of thousands with the Search Wing's anti-bomb lorry outside, snipers on the rooftops and local uniformed police parked and parading. It was a scenario that was doing little to reassure the public that nothing was going on.

The officer in charge was very pleased with how well things were going. I said, 'Yes, it couldn't be better. The minister's just changing his trousers. He can't believe all this is happening – and just for him.' I suggested that maybe some of the officers could be placed out of sight just to give an air of normality.

So our man was safe inside the ambassador's home. Exactly an hour later he wanted to go for a walk. We suggested Battersea Park, just on the other side of the Thames. This was the best option. A quiet walk to stretch the legs and a good time for him to get to know his team.

There are two things about impromptu events. I have to improvise proper security but on the other hand a spur-of-the-moment change of plan also catches the bad guys on the wrong foot.

The minister came out of the house and was quickly put into the car. The rule is that, once the principal's car door is closed, everyone should move, as the lead car will not wait. You have to be aware of what's going on around you regarding unusual movements but always keep one eye on the principal.

Both cars moved off and onto the Embankment. The drivers, not allowing any other vehicle to get between them, turned right, then left over Battersea Bridge, then left into Battersea Park. It was a warm and sunny day, ideal for a stroll in the late summer sunshine. The park was quiet, as most people were still at work. There was just the odd jogger on the footpaths but nothing to get worried about.

The minister walked ahead of me as Tony and Tim talked to him. We were all enjoying the walk away from prying eyes and the intrusion that comes with protection, when our peace was shattered.

The Met copter was whirling above us. The helicopter is equipped with a TV camera beaming the pictures back to Scotland Yard. Our movements were being monitored as always from GT. Tony looked up and then back at me with a nod. I took the hint and called Gold in GT.

'Can we please reassign India 99 [the copter]? I think that, in view of the sudden decision, he can be left alone to enjoy the walk.'

Gold said he wanted to see what was happening and India 99 gave him an overall picture of any unfolding events. We now had our first problem, not with any shots being fired but from a senior officer who wanted to have his finger in the pie. I said, 'No, call 99 off, we don't need it. All that it's doing is bringing us to everyone's attention and telling the world and its dog where we are. Call it off. Now!'

Thankfully we had our own senior SB officer in GT. A very brief discussion took place and India 99 flew away. Peace returned.

The minister told us all about how he was cracking down on the drug trade in Cyprus. It was something that was steadily getting worse and involving the British Army base. His efforts were starting to take effect.

That's why we and he knew that an assassination team were London. He was a brave man, willing to die for what he believed was right.

He asked that as much care be taken as possible in dealing with his wife. Our fear was of her being kidnapped and held for ransom. Luckily, her idea of a good time was to stay inside the official residence, not shop along Bond Street like so many diplomatic wives.

Back at the residence and inside the ring of steel, the target was better protected than our own Prime Minister. Tony stayed inside the house while I went home with the Friday evening commuting crowd from London's Charing Cross to Tonbridge in Kent, carrying my Glock and fifty rounds of ammunition. You never know who you're sitting next to on the train.

I didn't sleep that well. There were two assassination risk areas the next day, the first at a lecture at the University of London near Russell Square, now, of course, a sad tourist attraction since the 7/7 bombings in 2005. If we survived that there was an evening visit to the Greek Cypriot community in north London.

Before the off, I called GT and was told that the university had been searched early that morning. The students produced ID cards, but one snag was that this was a Saturday, so a high proportion of students were older. We had completed criminal-record checks on them as well as giving their names to MI5 for them to process on their database. Lecturers were also checked as well as the cleaners and ancillary staff. No flags went up.

As with all high-profile events, SB work closely with MI5, who take care of domestic security, as well as MI6, who deal with foreign concerns. Most of our embassies abroad have a resident spook working somewhere in the building just as foreign embassies have a spy in theirs. SB has its own indices as well, which we keep to ourselves, or at least we used to prior to 9/11.

There was much interdepartmental politics. SB jealously kept its secrets and informers from MI5, who did the same to us. SB would inform MI5 on security matters and they would tell us four-fifths and five-eighths of nothing.

Between the three main security organisations there was a lot of mistrust. SB had a liaison officer working in MI5's headquarters at Thames House on Millbank and, if he went to the bathroom, someone would time him. If he was longer than they thought appropriate then they would ask why. A spooky crowd in every sense.

We also had little faith in A4, the surveillance side of MI5. They sometimes followed and lost suspects. 'A4 have fucked up again' was a periodical rallying cry for us.

Yet that morning even they seemed to have done their jobs and, after a final check around the residence, I gave the OK to 'Go!'

Tony came out first and looked at me for a double check. He was closely followed by Zorba and Tim, our SB colleague who would travel in the car with me. Tim had no protection experience and wasn't even firearm-trained, so it was another complication, but one that I knew about and could deal with. India 99 hovered overhead to keep us company.

The journey from Cheyne Walk to just off Russell Square was not a long drive but was full of potential killing zones where the car had to stop or slow down. I had to be especially alert and concentrate. I knew we were being followed by 'our' side, but this made it difficult to pick out the killers. I hoped the bad guys didn't realise that a surveillance team was with us.

We carried encrypted radios, giving us secure communications with each other as well as GT, but with no one else. We needed to have the airways clear for emergencies.

I got a call that the assassination team had been located in London's West End close to our final destination. I told the lead car.

A covert firearms team were deployed to intercept the hit

men and, if necessary, reverse the situation and kill them. Things were beginning to get a little tense. This was, after all, in the centre of London and if our guys got it wrong there would be an almighty political storm.

I suggested that we drive around and keep our options open. If it all went wrong and an attack came in we could take off to the nearest police station and armour up.

What we didn't want was for them and us to meet at the university and have a shootout on the streets; that would be the worst possible scenario.

We slowed it down and waited for confirmation that the hit team had been stopped, dead or alive.

With our thoughts now racing away and with trying to keep things calm and away from the minister, I received another call. The surveillance team had lost them! Fucking great! Now what? I passed on the message to the lead car. There was just a sigh, and it wasn't one of relief.

At least we had some intel. We were now looking for a black BMW with four guys of Mediterranean appearance in it. Needle and haystack were a couple of the more polite words charging around in my brain.

The big question was, where were the would-be killers heading? I called GT and asked that question. I was told that they were travelling in the direction of Russell Square.

Should we cancel the event or keep going? We were heading for a possible shootout with casualties, probably involving innocent Londoners and tourists.

The teams at the university were ready and knew of the downturn in the situation – they were on action alert. I hoped that they were on better form than the surveillance unit.

The close-protection team consisted of a number of person

protection officers (PPOs) and specialist drivers, and we just had to get on with it. If we bottled it, that would send out all kinds of messages to any terrorist organisation that we were not up to the job – especially the Provisional IRA. It had not been that many months since the Canary Wharf bomb cracked wide open their supposed ceasefire. The February 1996 explosion in London's Docklands had got everybody's attention and personal security and other precautions – relaxed during the ceasefire – were back in force.

In that delicate and ever-dangerous atmosphere, I didn't want to be seen as backing off, and neither did the rest of the team. And we had our snipers on the roofs and police crawling all the vicinity, so it would have been stupid for anyone to mount an attack.

Wouldn't it? Yet, how desperate were these killers?

We had to match their determination, do our jobs and shoot it out with them. At least I would, while Tony tried to get the principal away from the gun battle.

But the principal never knew a thing. We didn't want him even more anxious than he already was; he could leave all the anxiety to us.

The cars moved closer to the venue. I called GT one more time to see if the surveillance teams had located the BMW. No, came the reply. This was it, no going back.

We turned the corner and approached the main entrance to the building. The only people inside the cordon were police officers. The cars pulled up outside and stopped. I got out and went to the steps and looked over to a colleague. 'All OK here?'

The rule is that the principal does not get out of the car until the PPO opens his door. The SB officer may have to push his charge back inside the car and dive on top of him or drag him to safety inside the building; these decisions have to be made in the blink of an eye. A wrong choice could result in the death of the principal and a very long inquiry.

Tony opened the door and the minister got out. Tony took up a position on his right shoulder and within arm's length of him. I walked slightly in front of him and led the way into the building looking for menace. There was one guy – looked like a student – standing by the notice board looking at the adverts. A uniformed officer was inside the building and looking at me. I glared back and pointed to the student. The officer snapped out of his daze and moved him away with some degree of force. I heard an argument start but didn't hang around for the conclusion.

As we went deeper into the building I noticed our search team officers on the doors to other rooms. Only one exit and entrance had been used, both monitored by an airport-style metal detector.

Tony stood close to the minister but to one side of the stage. Scattered around the auditorium were plain-clothes firearms officers trying to look interested in the speech. I stayed at the back. I needed to leave the room to make phone calls and make arrangements for our return. It seemed calm.

Yet we still had four men somewhere in London who wanted to kill a visitor to the capital, possibly killing many others in the process. I called GT to see if anything had come back about the BMW. I was told that it had come back as 'no trace'.

We now had to get home. We had to do it by the quickest route and not one that we had done in our preparations in case we had been followed earlier. Tony radioed that the speech was over and that he was making his way out. It would be the same in reverse, making sure that the students along our route could not interfere with our progress. I went ahead into the street and made sure it was as safe as we could hope for. I looked up and the snipers on the roof were leaning on the edge of their vantage points.

The cars had their engines running and the minister emerged from the building. He got into the car and the door closed. Tony got into the front passenger seat. Tim and I got into our car and we entered the Saturday-morning traffic. Our cars stayed close to one another, not allowing any vehicle to get between us. These were dangerous times and we were all ready for what might be thrown our way.

We had left the safety of our protectors and for the half-hour we were virtually on our own. India 99 was monitoring our progress. The journey took half an hour exactly, and, as we neared the residence, I called ahead to let the DPG know of our imminent arrival.

I saw lots of black BMWs but not, thankfully, the one with our hit team in. The surveillance teams that were following us checked out every BMW that came near us.

The firearms team had a 'hard stop' on one particular car, forcing it to brake and aiming MP5 9mm submachine guns at the occupants, yelling and shouting at them to get out of the car and lie on the ground. If anyone of them failed to comply there was a very real possibility that they would have been shot on the spot.

From the safety of the residence I told Gold in GT that the evening's event was even more of a threat as we were going into the Cypriot community, where an assassin could be waiting. This was not a time for doing half-measures. We had to be thorough and be seen to be thorough. The searching must be high-profile so that the world and his dog could see what the search teams were doing. In that way, we hoped that the killers would stay away and not attempt anything at the venue.

Which left, as always, the high danger of going to and from the meeting, and the time to drive arrived quickly. Tony came out first and I was already on the pavement standing by my car as he walked the minister out, and put him into the car. We moved off and left the comfort of our static armed protection, and made our way into London's Saturday-evening, theatre traffic.

We were driving through the busiest part of London. Traffic was heavy with cars trying to find places to park or just getting from one side of town to the other. Taxis were doing what they do best, getting in everyone's way, dropping people off, or picking them up and stopping wherever they could and blocking the free flow of traffic.

With so many cars it would be difficult for an attack to happen, unless the hit team had changed their plans and were using a motorbike; if so, it would be impossible to stop them or get a shot off at them without causing danger to the crowds.

When we arrived at the event it was clear we had a successful lockdown; we were secure. The event was a great success and it was time to go home. The BMW had not been seen again but that didn't mean that they were still using the same car. Any assassin would change vehicles on a regular basis to keep those protecting his mark on constant guard.

I thought that, with so much security, maybe they had decided not to kill in London. We had everything in place to defend ourselves against an attack and we were completely overt in all that we did, the idea being that they might have second thoughts about carrying out their plan. However, I knew things were not right. These guys had just disappeared.

They were supposed to be professionals and paid a lot of money to kill their target, but now they had gone. We seemed to have scared them off. Or had we?

With the minister safely in the house and the final checks to GT telling them that he was safe inside, it was time to get some rest and be ready for the return flight home late the next afternoon.

I arrived back at the Yard the next day to be told that there were no planned movements until the evening flight. We enjoyed Sunday lunch taken with a fine glass of Adam's ale, which is water. No alcohol on this job.

Time to remove the target from the UK. With the car doors closed, we moved off west along the A4 towards Heathrow. As a change, we went down the A40 and cut across the A312 towards the airport. I heard India 99 tracking our progress. This final drive would be the last chance the attackers had of killing Evangelos Yannopoulos.

As we approached the junction with the M4 I received a call from GT: did we still need the services of India 99? Air traffic control had stopped all flights in and out of Heathrow. That was astonishing – the government put such importance on our mission that all aircraft were on hold as India 99 was flying into the takeoff and landing safety zone.

I immediately cancelled the air surveillance and let the world carry on. A few seconds later the noisy helicopter peeled away and rattled its way back to a safe area as we drove towards Control Post 4 talking to Hunter 90, the armed airport police, who met us and escorted us to the Hounslow Suite. It seemed months, not days, since we'd last been there.

Special services said the plane was ready to board. We got back into the cars and were escorted to the stand. With a final goodbye, the minister and his wife boarded. Tim went on to say his final farewells. Moments later, Tim came off the plane with a look that I didn't like.

'They're on the fucking flight!'

'What do you mean?'

'The killers – they're on the fucking flight!'

I was, and must have sounded, astonished. 'What?'

'I've just checked the flight manifest and saw their names and looked at the seats. Four of them are on the flight!'

I thought for a moment and then relaxed. 'Well, there's no need to worry. We'll call Limassol and tell them the score. The flight's direct to Cyprus.'

I turned to the airport dispatcher and asked, 'This is a direct flight, isn't it?'

'No. It stops in Paris CDG – Charles De Gaulle.'

Answers somersaulted through my mind. That's why the gunmen backed off in town: they knew the flight details; they're going to do him in Paris, get him off the plane, kill him and vanish into the city.

We had to pull the target and his wife, who were at the sharp end of the plane, off the flight but without fuss. I got their bags off first.

I called GT and told them, and to a man they couldn't believe it. GT had to stay open for the night. With all the cover that we had over the last few days we were now back to doing things the SB way: low-profile and very low-key. We had no choice.

At the last possible moment – with the cabin crew standing in the gangway to hide what was going on – we took the minister and his wife off the aircraft. We hoped the gunmen didn't have someone on the outside to warn that their targets had been lifted.

We decided to go to one of the airport hotels, as there was a direct Monday-morning flight. At the hotel I asked for six rooms on the same floor. The check-in girl said they were full. I produced my warrant card and told her we were Special Branch and we needed the rooms. The duty manager did a lot of button-pushing and got us what we wanted.

I contacted the DPG and asked them to come out to provide overnight security while we tried to get some sleep. They said it was out of their area and that they couldn't provide cover. Everyone was tired and getting tense and nervous. I wasn't in the mood for this bollocks.

I called GT and angrily explained we needed overnight armed cover outside the target's room. We wanted it now! I also said that if the DPG couldn't find their way out of central London then maybe Heathrow police could help us. That was precisely what happened, and it was the most expedient solution. It was a short rest, as the flight left at 7 a.m. This time we checked the flight list and no one came to our notice. We said our final farewells again and they got on the plane. We waited for the doors to close so that we could finally relax.

It was taking a long time for this to happen, when the captain appeared. 'We have a malfunction in one of the engines,' he said. 'We may have to cancel the flight.'

I could have wept. It must be a conspiracy. I told GT and they too were speechless. It just wasn't in the script. We waited as the captain went down the stairs and, with the ground crew, checked one of the engines.

I looked out of the staircase window and saw the captain with a torch and a hammer. I nudged Tim and said with misplaced sarcasm, 'This should fix it.'

The pilot put his head into the engine and then reappeared and went back into the cockpit. Wonderfully, the cabin crew waved goodbye and closed the door. We waited for 'wheels up'. When it happened I called GT – the target had left UK soil alive.

We took ourselves and our guns and ammunition back to Scotland Yard. Job done.

Chapter Two
The Khyber Pass

'An eye for an eye only ends up making
the whole world blind.'
Mohandas Gandhi, 1931

Routine is deadly, and one of the laws of preventing assassinations is to avoid it. The regular, same place, same time, same day, each week, can be a killer. Or certainly enable one.

But it can't always be avoided. Prime Minister's Question Time is always at noon on a Wednesday at the House of Commons. SB always have to anticipate the worst.

It involves around 250 officers of the Metropolitan Police to get the PM safely from Downing Street to the Commons. Yet, while he's inside verbally jousting with the Leader of the Opposition, we're still at work.

On A Squad there were 'office' days between and during close-protection assignments.

Then, I would be asked to 'guest' on any number of protection jobs. In my early days in SB, I was flying by the seat of my pants – on some of my most precarious stints I hadn't even had bodyguard training – but in the months and years following 9/11 the security services and their operational techniques were dragged into the twenty-first century.

One aspect of that is Operation Kratos, the Met's anti-terrorist shoot-to-kill policy. There are all manner of rules, of etiquette if you like, about this. But if Kratos is engaged, and the order is given to shoot or a police gunman decides to pull the trigger, the target is going down, taken out. No question. Shot in the head. End of life.

But that's just the beginning of the story if anything goes wrong.

At intervals after 9/11, I was called in to monitor the crowds outside the House of Commons before, during and after Prime Minister's Questions. Specifically, I was watching for suicide bombers.

It was a tense, knife-edge of a job. Behind me, placed strategically on the roof of the Treasury building, were Met snipers. If I identified a threat then a commander like Deputy Assistant Commissioner Cressida Dick – who was media-roasted over the contentious 2005 shooting of Brazilian Jean Charles de Menezes, mistaken for a bomber and killed in Stockwell Tube station on the London Underground – could order it taken out.

Outside the Commons I would grasp the security railings with white knuckles for at my word someone could die. It might be that attractive girl who I believed had a bomb strapped around her. Or a guy lurking around and looking like danger.

The consequences – such as those following the de Menezes shooting, which are still going on – were a constant concern.

Every Wednesday at the Commons and all over the UK and

the world, there are officers involved in such intense surveillance, making life-and-death judgements.

I always felt more comfortable being in direct control of the action, for that way I would live or die by my own decisions. Of course, that can be a lonely tightrope to walk. Especially when you're involved in a carry-on up the Khyber Pass.

Throughout the 1990s, the operations of the security services, and therefore of my outfit, A Squad, had still worked in a quaint, old and (usually salmon-striped) school-tie sort of way. Armed protection, seen by many as all a bit of a bore, was only for senior ministers.

Yet now I, along with many other protection officers, was authorised to carry only a sidearm, a Glock 17. Because of 9/11 there was now an unholy rush to train all A Squad protection officers with the Heckler and Koch MP5 carbine – the lethal-looking one you see uniformed cops carrying at airports and other hot spots.

Urgent requests were made for immediate training, but crazily – given the tense international atmosphere – there were not enough qualified instructors to cope with the workload. In spite of being one of the longest-serving and most experienced officers, I was one of those who were not authorised to carry an MP5.

But I was packing my Glock, held safely in a plain leather holster. Leather was the best material because over time it moulded itself to the shape of the Glock which could be easily drawn from it.

On day-to-day jobs I was comfortable with that. But – and there's always a but in this business – in 2001, four weeks after the tragic events in New York, I was told that I had been selected along with three SB colleagues to accompany the

Birmingham Labour MP Clare Short, then Secretary of State for International Development, to Pakistan.

She wanted to see that the food and aid provided by the UK government for civilians caught up in George W Bush and Tony Blair's War on Terror was getting through the Khyber Pass into Afghanistan. I was told I was chosen for the perilous assignment because of my experience and calm manner. We found ourselves working in isolation without substantial support. Maybe the thought of Clare Short turning up anywhere in the world would be enough to scare anybody, including Osama bin Laden and al-Qaeda, so we didn't need the Who Dares Wins heavyweights.

The team leader, Paul, and another officer, Oliver, would go on ahead liaising with the British High Commissioner and the resident spook from MI6. They would carry MP5s, with Richard taking a cut-down Heckler and Koch MP5K for concealed carry – and a high rate of automatic fire. My sidekick Chris and I ordered up a hundred rounds of ammunition each. With their carbines and our Glocks and with the ammo, it appeared we were equipped to start our own war.

What was I letting myself in for? The nightmare was being taken hostage, tortured or worse. We had had no training about what to do in a hostage situation; we could hardly give our name, rank and serial number. I could be a very valuable asset: a Special Branch officer, police spy, and so far from home, too. I could be paraded in front of the world's media via Al Jazeera, the Arab news network, and milked for the propaganda.

Not much I could do about it. I packed. I had a small rucksack, which contained my gun and ammunition. Airline policy was that our weapons had to be unloaded and placed in a ballistic bag and the ammunition in another, similar, bag;

because of the recent horrors in the skies, our hardware was placed in the hold.

We were all off from Gatwick to Islamabad to help save the world, flying first-class. Ms Short and her principal private secretary sat in front of Bob and me. The steward asked what she would like to drink.

'What have you got?'

'We have champagne.'

'Oh, champagne would be lovely,' came the instant response.

Iain and Richard were waiting in the heat at Islamabad along with the British High Commissioner and the Pakistani security team. Bob and I signed a firearms certificate authorising us to carry our weapons in Pakistan.

We put our holsters on and, in the privacy of a small room in the airport terminal, loaded and cocked our guns ready for anything that might happen. I checked my other ammo magazines.

We returned to the main party and, once all our bags had been checked and passports stamped, we left the airport in a convoy of vehicles and headed straight for the High Commissioner's residence. It was a jittery ride all the way, with policemen at every junction stopping the traffic to let the convoy through without hindrance.

None of us knew how secure or trustworthy the Pakistani police were. Had they told anyone about our route? After all, this was a Muslim country and there was sympathy with al-Qaeda's cause. A war was being waged not that far away and here within their grasp was a prime target, a UK government minister and a secret policeman. What a ball.

I kept my hand close to my Glock. Road movements are

notoriously treacherous and I wasn't going to be unprepared if we were attacked.

The convoy, sirens wailing and the backup cars swerving all over the road keeping other cars from getting into the convoy, kept up high speed all the way to the residence. Most of the police had AK-47s with the barrels sticking out of the opened windows. A couple of cars came out of side roads without looking, almost crashing into the embassy vehicle Bob and I were in. Bad driving, or something more sinister? I gripped my Glock more firmly.

There were machine-gun posts on each side of the road and soldiers patrolling near the residence, which stood behind bulletproof gates in the diplomatic quarter of the city. That banged home the thought that I was in the middle of a very high threat with a pistol that had a maximum range of about 25 metres and a hundred rounds of 9mm. The terrorists had AK-47s with high-velocity ammo and an effective range of more than twice that distance.

The next day we waved the flag announcing we were there. Ms Short had a meeting with President Pervez Musharraf, and, to get the government's message across that we were here to help the people of Afghanistan, she did TV and radio interviews. After the drama of 9/11, the bad guys were given another prime target, and this time closer to home. I was the advance man, going off to each venue to make sure all the security arrangements were in place; as soon as the official party arrived I would be off to the next meeting. This was a one-man job. I had a driver, gun, ammo and a mobile phone. My gun was loaded and magazines were in every pocket.

I was wearing a shoulder holster rather than one attached to my trouser belt. In the sitting position it would take longer to draw my gun from my belt. With a shoulder holster my gun is under my left arm and I can draw it, aim and fire in less than two seconds.

That first day, trying to anticipate possible threats somewhere among all the noise and dust and aromas of a strange, exotic city, there were difficult moments with the crowds and the masses of media, especially during our courtesy call on President Musharraf.

After a tense, scary and long, hot day, the early-evening drinks should have cooled us all down. No such luck. The Secretary of State wanted to go up the Khyber Pass, right on top of the Taliban.

And vice versa.

She'd decided she needed to see that the aid was getting through. We all nearly choked on our gin and tonics. OK, we could do the impossible, but the suicidal! She wanted to see the food mountain, meet the drivers and get as close as possible to where the aid lorries were being stopped by terrorists.

The more the problems that were pointed out, the stroppier she became about getting her way. It was decided that she could go to visit the World Food Programme (WFP) depot at Peshawar on the North-West Frontier.

Ms Short was going to fly up. I would have to go on ahead by road alone. There wasn't much of a briefing – what could anybody say? There were no instructions for a trip like this.

Iain presented me with a satellite phone. It was the size of a briefcase. He opened it and explained how it worked. It took some time, but, after twisting it one way and then the other, we found the best signal. It worked perfectly. At least I could call for help – if I wasn't in a hurry!

The phone and the rest of the gear went into a bulletproof

white GMC Suburban sedan – supplied by the US Embassy, because the British Embassy didn't have an armoured vehicle available – and I met my two WFP guides, good guys: Ahmed, an Afghan, and Mohammed, a Pakistani. Ahmed was going to drive

We were on the road to Peshawar when, instinctively, I checked if we were being followed; silly, what was the point? We were driving straight into the lions' den. They didn't need to follow us.

The bombing of besieged Afghanistan had sent thousands of refugees into Pakistan. The border was not secure and genuine refugees had been infiltrated by Taliban fighters; it was a powder keg of a place, all the passion and unrest ready to blow up at any minute.

The journey was surprisingly smooth and we made good time out of the city. Shanty towns were being left behind and replaced by small collections of mud huts, the locals sharing them with snakes, spiders and mosquitoes – and not a lot of hope.

On the roads some cars displayed black-and-white flags showing support for Osama bin Laden and al-Qaeda. It made me nervous – and angry – to see these vehicles openly cheering on a terrorist organisation that had just murdered more than three thousand people.

We were going through small villages and I was aware we were the centre of attention. It then hit me like a brick in the face. I said to Ahmed, 'This vehicle was borrowed from the Americans, yes? Do we have American diplomatic plates still on the vehicle?'

'Yes, we do.'

I had been so concerned with the satellite phone that I had forgotten a simple but vital detail. I was going into a war zone with an American car displaying American diplomatic number plates. We were waving the Stars and Stripes in the face of the Taliban.

At the next village we found a café for lunch, where, bizarrely, all the customers were watching a rerun of the 1998 World Cup final between France and Brazil. I was enjoying the rice when I heard gunfire nearby. I put my hand under my jacket and released the thumb-catch ready to get out of the place. I told Ahmed to get the car started and the others to go in front of me. Another two shots went off. There was some automatic fire. In the hills there were crowds of armed men. Bursts of automatic fire went off again. They were waving their weapons in the air and pointing in our direction. Shit!

I told Ahmed to drive slowly away from the shots and the hostile band. Screaming tyres wouldn't have helped the situation. Better to be calm but I hoped it wasn't a trap sending us into an ambush.

Ahmed knew the territory and took us to a safe house, a white colonial-style building. Mohammed had called ahead and the gates were already open as we swept into the drive. I got the phone to work and told the main delegation that it was like the Wild West and the Secretary of State's visit was too risky, that the whole thing should be cancelled. With all this going on I was glad that I had a Glock with a maximum of 25 metres – it was very reassuring to know I had sufficient firepower. If only.

The answer came back that Clare Short was going to Peshawar no matter what. She was not going to be intimidated!

But I was to press on, chin up. The world order was very volatile, with Christian and Muslim pitted against each other for the glory of whatever god you happen to believe in. Then there were politicians playing politics and saying that what they were doing was right and they were the ones who had the solution to it all. In the middle of this mayhem were people like me trying to do a job and make some sense of it.

This was so different from fighting the IRA or hit men, evil guys who didn't want to be caught, let alone killed; then along came this lot who want to die so they can go and meet Allah and seventy-two virgins. What chance did any of us have against that kind of mindset?

The hell with it! We broke cover and headed for the air force base where the Secretary of State would arrive. Four other vehicles turned up from the World Food Programme to help out with transport. I looked to the skies, not only for her arrival but for divine inspiration. This was going to be fraught with danger. I only hoped no one from the WFP had told their friends who was coming to visit.

I heard the approaching military aircraft before I saw it. It was an old Sea King and not in its prime. I guessed that, if the Pakistani Air Force were going to lose a helicopter, it had better not be a new one, diplomatic visitor or not.

With everyone on the ground I set off for the WFP depot, a collection of well-maintained offices and a large warehouse containing a mountain of food sacks ready to be transported over the border to Afghanistan.

A little further on were about twenty brightly painted lorries all waiting to be loaded with the aid. Dozens and dozens of drivers were sitting around the site. I couldn't see any security guards or any signs of protection. I was told that this was a humanitarian effort and that any sign of military or armed guards would give the wrong message.

I was not comfortable with the total lack of security, but

what could I do? I had already said that this was nuts but the government minister's image was everything and, just as I was thinking all this, a television crew arrived. The drivers swamped the TV people; it was all going down the pan. I ushered the crew away from the drivers and back to the main gate to await the arrival of the guest of honour.

The convoy swept in through the gates and stopped outside the main offices. With a quick hello and a smile to the gathered photographers, Clare Short toured the compound. As she approached the trucks, all the drivers stampeded towards her. I moved in to prevent her from being crushed. She glared at me with anger. 'What are you doing? You're going to getting in the way of the photo opportunity. I don't want you in the way, we must get our message out!'

I snarled back, 'Your precious message is putting all our lives at risk and I am going to do all that I can to keep everybody alive!'

We were both looking daggers at each other. I wasn't going to back down.

'Just stay out of the way!'

'You do the smiling and I'll take care of the shooting if it starts.'

The TV crew and the drivers all gathered around Ms Disgruntled, who at once turned on the full charm offensive. I tried to look at the dangers. Who was carrying a knife? Well, most of them. She managed to get onto the loading bay, so she was at a good vantage point to be filmed, photographed – and shot from her good side.

I stood to one side so that I had a clear view of the whole scene as well as having a clear shot if needed. The drivers and the press were by now up close and personal. We had to push them back to make a safety gap. My other two team members could not get involved with the crowd scenes as they were carrying carbines and needed a wider arc of fire.

Ms Short was by now in full flow, extolling the virtues of her department. The Secretary of State wanted the drivers somewhere in the picture to show that she was at the front line and at one with their struggle. It was all so phoney, like many such occasions I've witnessed.

I have seen how government, of all persuasions, works, and it's all very cynical. But I have to say that the Blair government was by far the most despicable of the lot. It relied solely on focus groups, telling the electorate what they wanted to hear and doing completely the opposite.

Clare Short had stopped preaching and we went back to the main WFP buildings for a final meeting. It was here I was told a border refugee camp visit been cancelled by the Pakistani government because of rioting by Taliban supporters. Their security said she could be killed if news that she was travelling there got out. It would have put her life in jeopardy. But the Secretary of State still wanted to go. We were all getting a little sick and tired of her attitude.

We couldn't go by road because of distance and security, and then someone in the brains department decided she could fly over the camp. I was to accompany her in the old Sea King copter. The rotor blades started and the whole thing started to vibrate and rattle. The Pakistani security team, who had been telling me earlier about the Taliban's surface-to-air missiles, were waving us goodbye. Wisely, they were staying on the ground.

As we flew over the barren land towards the Pakistani–Afghan border, the copter shot out flares to divert heat-seeking missiles. Our bone-shaker was circling the refugee camp. The noise and the heat inside were becoming unbearable. The longer we stayed over this sea of unrest the more risk we were being exposed to. The Secretary of State was genuinely shocked by the size of the camp, and that made me feel better about her.

Eventually, we arrived back in Islamabad. With everyone safe, I gave the Pakistani police souvenirs of our visit: Metropolitan Police badges, paperweights and plaques.

Then we were off with heightened Pakistani security and soon en route, first-class, to Gatwick with our guns and the ammunition, not a round fired, which, in the circumstances, was a good if surprising result, in the land where so many are in a rush to get to heaven.

Chapter Three
Gun Law

'You Never Can Tell'

Chuck Berry song title, 1964

The intricacies of sophisticated, high-level, practised protection – everything from first aid for someone you've shot to intelligence-gathering, gunmanship and evasive driving – were not something I gave a thought to as I was growing up in Lewisham in southeast London. Or the fate of world leaders. I wanted to be a professional golfer.

Yet policing was in the family. My parents met in Lee Green police station. My father's sister was married to a copper and lived in a police flat within the station. On the other side of the station yard was another apartment, where a Scottish couple lived. They became my aunt and uncle after my mother came down from Hamilton in Scotland for a holiday and met and married my dad.

There wasn't a lot of money but plenty of love growing up. School life was good. I didn't excel but I wasn't thick either, just lazy. I got two GCE O-levels: technical drawing and geography. The problem was I'd discovered golf. I was also in the school football team and I even had a trial with Charlton, but it didn't come to anything.

I left school armed with my two O-levels and a single-figure golf handicap. My dad suggested I join the police. I had two uncles in the force, one of them a senior-ranking officer in Croydon, the other working in the information room at Scotland Yard. My cousin was also in the job, so I was not afraid of policemen. However, at seventeen, I thought I was too young – and I wanted time on the golf course.

I became a postman, starting work early and on the course by lunchtime. So, six days a week, I started to walk the mean streets of Beckenham, Kent. After five years and having just married I realised I couldn't be a postman for the rest of my life. In those days there were plenty of vacancies in the police and I was invited to Paddington Green Police Station for the entrance exam, which went fine.

The ordeal was the medical. We'd been told to bring a dressing gown and a pair of slippers, both of which I didn't own. I was the only prospective recruit who had the items just out of the wrapper.

I went in front of three doctors and was told to strip naked. This was novel, standing in front of three men stark bollock naked while they looked me up and down. The guy in the middle asked me to cough.

I said, 'I'm OK, I don't have a cough.'

He repeated his request without a smile, so I coughed. None of them were looking at me but staring at my 'orchestra stalls'. Having satisfied them that I could cough, they then asked me to turn around and bend over and touch my toes. They seemed to like what they saw and so I passed the medical. All that was left was the selection board.

My Uncle Bill – honest! – who was now in charge at Croydon police station, had fully briefed me on what to expect. He told me that there would be two senior officers; one would be pleasant and the other would play Mr Nasty to find out if I had a suspect or volatile temperament.

It went according to type. One officer was rude and aggressive in his questioning. After about five minutes of this he was looking through my application form and noticed the name of my uncle. 'You're the nephew of Bill Frame?'

I nodded. He then turned to the other man and said, 'As far as I'm concerned, no further questions. Bill Frame was my inspector at Notting Hill.'

It was my first but not only encounter with the old boys' network. I was a member of the Metropolitan Police, sixteen weeks' initial training to start at Hendon Police College in north London on 11 June 1979.

Thirty years later I'm carrying a gun and am a close-protection officer, albeit one serving the interests of private enterprise. It seems a lifetime away from pounding the beat on the streets of Croydon and then on traffic patrol working in Lambeth, Southwark and London's West End. It's been an eventful journey, one that truly began on a high-powered motorcycle.

I'd had a few years roaring about the streets of London when I joined the Special Escort Group (SEG), a small group of trained and armed motorcyclists taken from traffic patrol but also from the Diplomatic Protection Group.

The SEG comprises highly motivated and skilled riders who escort an eclectic group of people and property, from Category A villains to senior members of the royal family (I once protected the Queen's art collection from gallery to gallery) and visiting heads of state.

In the mid-1980s the main threat was the IRA and the unpredictable madmen and zealots wanting to headline their causes. Before I was officially on the team, I was ordered to learn how to use a gun on a two-week residential course at Lippetts Hill, a camp in the middle of Epping Forest in Essex.

It was a former wartime POW camp and all the huts were still standing and in use as classrooms and dormitories, while others had been converted into areas to teach armed search techniques.

The first gun I handled was a 4in Smith & Wesson Model 10 six-shot revolver. It seemed heavy but weighed only 32 ounces – just 907 grams. It was as I was holding and aiming that revolver that the total actuality of it hit home: I was being trained to shoot to stop a man. That was the policy before the age of Kratos. Only to stop, not to kill. To kill would be murder and against the law.

My group went to the back of the firing range and a red light came on indicating we were 'live'. The shoots were done from the 'drawn-weapons position': the weapon out and held at stomach level. Once the targets turned, you would then bring it up in front of you and either aim or, by using 'sense of direction', fire.

Sense-of-direction shooting was close-quarters shooting from 7 metres or less, and most assassinations are carried out at that range. It's where you don't have time to aim, you just 'punch the weapon out' and, staring at the target, fire. In theory, if you have a firm grip on the gun the bullets will hit the mark.

We were taught to 'double-tap' – fire two shots at the target. When the first bullet hits the body it causes a ripple effect and sends the body into a 'shock'. The next round enters the body and because the body has gone into spasm the bullet penetrates deeper.

Many of the photographs we were shown during the two weeks were of dead bodies. We were told that it wasn't the entry wound that caused the most damage – it's small and can be hard to locate – but the exit wound. As the bullet goes through the body it causes a wave effect, dragging flesh and body parts, and when it exits the wound is nearly always fatal.

We had stimulating, if that's the word, classroom discussions – one about shooting someone in the back. The scenario was that an officer turned out to an armed robbery and saw a man running down the street from the bank. Shots had been fired and he had a gun in his hand. Could you shoot him? Our chief instructor stopped the heated argument with, 'You can shoot him lots and lots of times. Shots will have been fired he still has a gun, and therefore still poses a threat to the public. Who knows what he might do next to avoid capture? So shoot him and possibly save someone's life. He chose to go out with a gun. It wasn't compulsory.'

Oh, if only it were always so cut and dried! I had to pass the final shoots to see if I had the skills to carry a gun. It was a timed, seventy-round shoot firing from 7 metres, 15 metres and 25 metres. The most difficult shoot is from 15 metres. We would have to fire six rounds, reload, fire another six rounds, and all in twenty seconds. It sounds easy but in practice, and with the pressure, it's not.

A pass was 85 per cent and above. We all took a box of 70 rounds and put them into our overall pockets and went down to the firing point. It was cold and, although the range was covered and dry, it had an open roof to allow the cordite to disperse. Our cold hands meant we all had problems with our dexterity in reloading our guns. But as the concentration and the adrenalin kicked in, I warmed up.

We all stood there with both hands gripping our guns, waiting for the targets to turn. Then they all turned. Punch out. Stop. Check. Bang, bang. Cover the target until they turn away. Targets turn away. Relax into the ready stance. Targets turn – and the same thing as before, always remembering to stop and check that the gun is being held steady. It is a proven fact that the first shot nearly always misses. A worrying statistic.

That's why we were taught that, when we are in the aim position, we should stop and check that the weapon is steady before firing.

From 7 meters I was doing OK, letting only the odd shot miss the target. I was becoming more confident, a major factor in shooting and in handling the gun. My fingers were working well in the reloading of the pistol and, with it, the speed in bringing the gun up ready to fire was getting faster. The action of pulling the trigger was also becoming smoother; a firm, steady movement keeps your grouping tighter on the target.

We were then moved back to 15 metres. It doesn't seem a lot but, having got used to firing from 7 metres, it felt like a long way. The principles were the same, but this time, instead of shooting by sense of direction at the target, it would be two aimed shots – again from the drawn-weapons position. We still had three seconds to come up into the aim posture and fire the shots, but even more important now was to stop and check, then fire.

I was not comfortable with the standard police stance of standing square on the target with the gun held in both hands in front of you. To me it was awkward. I was becoming concerned with this approach. One of the other students stood in the 'weaver' position, side on with the weapon an extension of his arm. I tried it and immediately felt more comfortable.

The final shoot was from was from 25 metres, and we were at the back of the range and at the maximum effectiveness of the gun. Twelve rounds with a reload after six, all to be done inside ninety seconds.

It wasn't just the time: it was the nature of this shoot. Wooden supports were placed in the ground to give us stability. We had to fire two shoots unsupported, two shots supported (placing the back of your left had against the support helped you keep the weapon steady), then two kneeling. In this position we would reload. Then two supported kneeling and finally two in the prone position.

This was not double-tapping but two carefully aimed shots, taking our time between the two. We were given a reference point on the target to aim for so that the shot would hit centre mass.

My first attempt was horrendous: I got only six shots in the target; the others were outside the outline and didn't score. If you cut the line around the target, then it would count. A few of my shots were still rising over Epping Forrest!

The two shots unsupported were the worst. With the nerves and concentration required, the gun was wavering all over the place. I needed to stay calm, and the way to do this was to move quickly between the different positions; in that way I would have more time to steady myself and hit the target. The other tough part of the routine was the two shots in the prone position. This was not easy because you had to fire slightly up at the target. You couldn't rest your hands on the floor because the gun would 'jump' when fired, so you had to raise the weapon slightly.

The test that would decide whether we were to become AFOs – authorised firearms officers – came in a final round of shoots. To make things more competitive, each of us put a pound into the kitty and the person with the highest score would win the lot.

I wasn't interested in the kitty: I wanted to pass this final hurdle. We knew that we could drop only ten shots out of seventy. I knew what my best shoots were, obviously the closer the better. The 25-metre shoot would be the toughest one in this shooting session.

We started from 7 metres and I stood on the firing line, hardly hearing as the range orders were yelled out. My nerves were now playing havoc as I stood there, weapon drawn and waiting for the targets to turn. I was taking long, slow, deep breaths to reduce my heart rate, and waited.

Then the targets turned. Up. Stop. Check. Pull the trigger as smoothly and as quickly as possible in one movement. My two shots went off down the range. Bollocks! I could see one had missed the target out of the circle! This was not in the game plan. The first shoot and I'd missed and dropped a shot. I knew that the hardest shoots were to come.

I had been shooting OK from 15 metres but I had to make sure that I kept it going. Again the range orders were given and, calming myself, I thought about the drills, keeping the trigger action smooth and holding the gun firmly without gripping so tight that my arms became tense.

A perfect score. Now I could settle down and relax a little. The others on the course were doing well and no one was in trouble with their scores. All the other shoots were going according to plan and it was looking as if I would qualify. All I had to do now was safely negotiate the final shoot from 25 metres.

I was in the second detail watching the other students and

waiting for my turn. The first detail counted their scores, put patches over the holes and now it was my turn. The range orders were given and I was quickly in position and taking aim, fired the first shot, steadied, then the second, then into the supported mode, fired again. It was all flowing nicely at a steady pace. I moved from one position to the other, quickly giving myself extra valuable seconds in which to take aim. The range officer called out, 'Thirty seconds!'

I had plenty of time, firing my last two shots with seconds to spare. I came into the kneeling stance and cleared my weapon, holding it so that it could be checked and I could be told it was safe and holster up.

The range officer called, 'Line clear. Forward and check.'

The moment of truth. I walked slowly down to the targets. I counted mine. All there. I'd done it. The relief was immense. I'd dropped only two shots out of seventy, but I didn't win the kitty. I was not bothered by that – I'd passed.

From then on I had to go every month to the Metropolitan Police firearms gurus to reclassify, to keep my AFO status; little did I know then that I'd be doing that for the next eighteen years.

My AFO rating gave me a big advantage when I joined Special Branch in November 1990.

Two of my mates in the traffic police had joined the Branch and I was keen to move on too. I knew there were no vacancies but I applied, hoping to pre-order an opportunity, as it were. It was well timed. SB's Operation Octavian, their ongoing struggle against the Provisional IRA, had discovered an assassination agenda in a house in Clapham, south London.

This IRA hit list prompted the recruitment of more officers

for A Squad. Round-the-clock static protection had been offered to scores of prominent people and SB urgently needed officers to provide it.

Within three weeks of applying, I had joined Special Branch. On my first day after a formal meeting with my chief superintendent, I went to the sixteenth floor of Scotland Yard to an area manned 24/7 by SB and Anti-Terrorist Branch officers. The armourer appeared and took me to a store cupboard that held dozens of revolvers. He checked the gun book and found a Smith & Wesson revolver: number 2566.

He made a new sheet with my name on it and I signed for my gun. No one else would use that particular pistol.

I kept this cumbersome gun in my holster for the next four years until Special Branch introduced the Austrian Glock 17. Apart from the barrel, it's made of plastic and is lighter and easier to conceal under your jacket and also during travel, even in the air, which is something that goes on regularly, if unknown to airport and airline authorities.

The Glock is now the first choice of security services worldwide. I went back to Lippetts Hill to be retrained on this semiautomatic, which has tritium sights and a very light, almost hair-trigger action compared with the revolver. The sights were illuminated so you could aim in low light. On the revolver we'd painted the rear sight red to try to get the same effect but it helped only a little.

It was a Dirty Harry scenario. Jacket on, I had to draw from the shoulder holster. I'd learned to keep some bullets or a bunch of keys in my jacket's side pocket: as you sweep the jacket out of the way the weight carries it behind you and you can get to your gun.

On the range the targets turned and in one movement I

flicked my jacket out of the way, got a good grip on the weapon and pulled it out, up into the aim, stop, check, bang, bang. Two shots, centre mass of the target. In two seconds. Jeez! I was impressed.

On the conversion course from the bulky Smith and Wesson revolver to the slimline Glock, I was taught how to get shots away more quickly. Once the trigger's pulled and the shot fired, I had to release the trigger fully and the Glock would start its mechanism to gather another bullet. On a click, the gun would be ready to fire again. I practised this endlessly and when I mastered it I could double-tap speedily. My accuracy improved immensely.

I returned to the Yard and went again to the sixteenth floor and asked the armourer for my new weapon. I went to the other side of the corridor and into a now bulletproof room to which only the armourer had access.

This plain office was much more secure. One recent Saturday morning the detective inspector in charge of the office asked for the keys to the armoury. He was not firearms-trained and there was no need for him to have access to the keys. But, being a senior officer, he was given them. The DI walked into the store, loaded a gun and shot himself dead.

There were new rules. The armourer inspected my 'pink ticket', a credit-card-sized piece of stiff paper that dictated the type of weapon I was authorised to carry, and showed that my monthly classifications were up to date. He handed me a Glock – number ATP2655 – and made out an issuing page in the binder. I signed for the gun, which I carried on all my future assignments.

In the early days of my training, being so much younger, I was very blasé about the life-and-death issues. After all, we were being trained to kill a common enemy, and I had no conscience about killing another man.

I joined the 'job' in Maggie's era; I was one of Thatcher's boys, to whom she had given a 40 per cent pay rise as soon as she'd come into power in 1979. We had never been governed by a prime minister like her before and I doubt that we will ever again. Most of us in the police thought that she was simply magnificent; in those days I never dreamed that I would become her protection officer.

Then there was the PIRA – the Provisional IRA, the Provos. As Prime Minister, Thatcher stood up to terrorism, having let the 1981 hunger striker Bobby Sands die in Northern Ireland's Maze Prison, in his own way, along with others.

But she had spoken out against the IRA before she became Prime Minister, and revenge from that organisation and other Republicans was merciless. Not long after I joined the police, a group called the Irish National Liberation Army (INLA) had murdered Airey Neave in March 1979. He had been a war hero and had escaped from Colditz, but was then Shadow Northern Ireland Secretary. Just weeks before Thatcher won the general election and became Prime Minister, the INLA had placed a highly sophisticated bomb in his car, which went off as he drove up the exit ramp of the House of Commons car park. A timing device and 'trembler' – which detonates the bomb through movement – were used to ensure a timed kill.

I still remember Maggie's reaction: 'He was one of freedom's warriors. Courageous, staunch, true. He lived for his beliefs and now he has died for them.'

Just before I joined A Squad in 1990, Ian Gow, who was

Thatcher's permanent private secretary, was killed. He had refused to take anything more than routine security precautions, yet knew he was an IRA assassination target. The IRA had planted a 4 1/2-pound Semtex bomb under his Montego car, which exploded as he reversed out of the driveway of his east Sussex home. Like Airey Neave, he died because he was 'a close personal associate of Margaret Thatcher', according to the IRA.

(Between Airey Neave and Ian Gow, there had also been the bomb at Tories' 1984 Brighton conference, and that would haunt me later.)

We also went to take on the miners' leader Arthur Scargill's flying pickets in the 1984–5 strike, when the country lurched from one crisis to another and she stood firm. I was later told by Ken Clarke, when he was the Tory Home Secretary in 1992–3, that she had known that at some stage she would have to take on the National Union of Mineworkers, and told the electricity boards (then still nationalised bodies) to stock up on coal; Scargill was doomed from the start. Not one piece of legislation she brought in on trade unions has been repealed.

When I started my firearms training and when I subsequently retrained, I always felt that the Prime Minister was definitely on my side and that I was one of her soldiers standing up for freedom and against tyranny.

I was trained to kill and my skills were constantly being enhanced to make me better at killing. I could be relied upon to protect people in a discreet and professional way, to be one of the crowd, but, when called upon, to step out of the crowd and kill with one shot, maybe two, and put a bullet in someone's head, a new aspect of training following the events of 9/11.

The only problem was the law. Once the threat had been removed, I as a police officer had a duty of care under health-and-safety legislation to care for my victim and give him first aid. If I didn't, and he died because I didn't put a plaster on a wound, I would be taken to court for manslaughter – not for shooting him but for not giving him first aid.

This bastard would have just tried to kill me or a senior politician (from whichever country), and now I had to give him first aid. We now have to kill terrorists in a humane way. The right to life is a fundamental right my arse! What happened to my right to life?

However, over the years, with all this legislation against those of us who were charged with protecting not only politicians but the general public, it was becoming more of a concern for me. Is it worth it? Of course it is, but the goalposts keep moving, and the law of the gun keeps changing. It's different, much greyer. When you are young the danger and the consequences of your actions don't seem to matter. When you're older and wiser, your views change and you recognise that many political ideals have been downgraded to notions that are often optional.

In this game it's a question of kill or be killed, and I have no problem about killing a guy who is about to kill me; but it's the aftermath that is of concern for me and many others on the firing line.

No one in their right mind glories in taking a life, and I am no exception. It's something I still wrestle with but do you know what? Insh'allah. That translates from Arabic as 'God willing' or 'if it is God's will'. It's not mine.

I was about to learn a great deal about the Muslim world and especially 'insh'allah'. It's an advantage to have God on side and many millions are convinced they do in an increasingly violent struggle to impact their beliefs on us. For me, one of the first huge challenges I had on A Squad was that half the world also believed Allah wanted them to murder the man I was assigned to protect.

But first I was to see the devastation of fury and bullets closer to home.

Chapter Four
Bloody Revenge

'They are at war with us. They come out with the
weapons of war – guns, bombs and missiles. They are
thugs, cowardly thugs, using guns and bombs against
innocent people.'

Margaret Thatcher, 1990, on the IRA

Going into the house gave me a chilling feeling. Bullet
holes were still in the walls of the drawing room and
dried blood was spattered around them and on the floor
where Sir Peter Terry had lain. The living room was much the
same, another page of the horror story, with bullet holes on
the far wall and the solid-oak cabinet riddled with entry and
exit holes.

It brought home to me the nature of the job I was expected
to do. I'd seen the result of injuries from bombs and bullets,
but nothing compares to the dispiriting sight of the aftermath
of an assassination. This was the sheer brutality of the
Provisional IRA and hammered home yet again what they
were capable of.

Air Vice-Marshal Sir Peter Terry was Governor-General of
Gibraltar in 1988 when three members of an IRA terror group
were killed by the SAS in what became known as the 'Death

on the Rock' shootings. It was a major blow to the IRA, as the trio were all senior operators in its European network.

Sir Peter was briefed about a plot to cause carnage outside Government House during a military ceremony. He was told that during Operation Flavius, a major intelligence operation involving police and MI5, a Provisional IRA Active Service Unit (ASU) had been followed across Europe and onto Gibraltar. The SAS had been deployed and were planning an ambush to stop them. Sir Peter signed the order for the soldiers to take out the terrorist team.

Once the SAS are involved, there will be no prisoners, and that turned out to be the case.

Since Sir Peter was approaching retirement, he asked the Foreign and Commonwealth Office (FCO) if he was under any threat from the IRA because of his actions; did he need to take any security precautions? The FCO said there were no concerns.

He returned to his home in Milford in Cannock Chase, Staffordshire. It was there, after supper on 18 September 1990, that he was sitting in his drawing room doing the Daily Telegraph crossword. His wife Betty and daughter Liz were in the living room putting photographs into an album.

Outside was an IRA ASU. The rear of the house looked over open farmland with public footpaths running through the fields. The lights were on, the curtains were not drawn, and Sir Peter was in clear view.

The ASU stood in the garden of his home and opened fire. They couldn't miss. Four shots of the twenty fired from their AK-47 hit him in the head and body, leaving nine wounds. The shots shattered his jaw and face and ripped into his body, narrowly missing his vital organs. Two of the bullets were 2mm from the brain, the thickness of a cornflake away.

Some of the rounds went through plasterboard walls, smashing through the oak furniture. Because Lady Terry and her daughter were sitting on the floor poring over the family photographs, the shots screamed over their heads and through a window. Splinters hit Lady Terry near her eyes.

Thinking that they had carried out a successful assassination, the ASU escaped across the farmland. But, immediately after the attack, a neighbour, luckily a doctor, ran into the house and stopped the blood flooding out of Sir Peter. That saved his life.

The other fortunate factor was that the killer was standing too close to his target – the bullets hadn't reached their maximum velocity. If the gunman had been 20 yards further back, the bullets would have gained deadly speed and Sir Peter would have died instantly.

He was in hospital for a number of weeks. His wounds had to be kept open to make sure all the debris from the bullets had been removed and so avoid gangrene. Lady Betty was lucky not to lose the sight of an eye and she made a full recovery.

Statements were taken from Liz Terry soon after the attack but, with hindsight, this was a mistake. Six months later she remembered that a man in camouflage jacket and a mask calmly walked out of the garden opposite, crossed the road and went into the field to make his escape. That hit-man was there in case Sir Peter saw the attack and ran out of the front of the house, where he'd have been assassinated.

Now, the Foreign Office decided to close the stable door and give Sir Peter protection. He was moved to the Royal Navy base in Cannock. He was given senior officer's quarters, which amounted to a four-bedroomed, semidetached house, with me and the rest of his protection team in the house that was the other half of the semi.

Once a week I would go round to check their home, which, for insurance reasons, had not been repaired. It sharpened my awareness of what is required. It is only natural that at times we can become casual – 'nothing will happen today' – but this gruesome scene put into sharp focus the possibility that it just might, and I'd better always be prepared for it.

They were a fantastic, remarkable couple. When the house was finally made good and Sir Peter and Lady Terry had the mental strength to return, we protection boys would help out by cutting the grass and taking his car out. We would sit in the garden with them and have tea and cake. They never settled back into the house, but sold it and moved away from the area.

The assassination attempt on Sir Peter heightened security and our workload. VIPs, ranging from politicians to armed services commanders and civil servants, were warned to be prepared for terror attacks. Sir Charles Tidbury, the chairman of Whitbread and a leader of the British brewing industry, was most certainly a target.

His name was one of the more than two hundred found on the list at the IRA hideout and bomb factory in Clapham. There seemed little reason for it. He'd been an army intelligence officer but had never served in Ulster and was not particularly close to Margaret Thatcher.

We discovered that his one significant offence, in Republican eyes, had been to accept the chairmanship of the William and Mary Tercentenary Trust, which was formed to raise money to mark the anniversary of the Glorious Revolution of 1688. Although the celebrations carefully avoided any reference to William of Orange's subsequent triumph over Irish Catholics at the Battle of the Boyne, the IRA bracketed Tidbury with several former Northern Ireland government ministers.

Which was why he was under the care of A Squad.

On 15 September 1990, SB officers guarding Tidbury's farmhouse in Hampshire disturbed two armed intruders, causing them to take off in a blue Ford Sierra. It was discovered in the car park at Stonehenge two weeks later; its occupants, Pearse McAuley and Nessan Quinlan, were charged with conspiracy to murder and jailed.

Later that year, when I became part of his protection, it was clear he was at serious risk – and my partner and I nearly drove him into an IRA mortar attack.

We had a meeting at Barclays Bank at the old Royal Mint Buildings by Tower Bridge. The winter had set in and snow was settling, one of those days the advertising men like, and, with Sir Charles happily sitting in the armoured Jag, we came up Victoria Street, past Scotland Yard and around Parliament Square.

My partner Simon had decided he wanted to go up Whitehall and along the Embankment to Lower Thames Street. As we negotiated Parliament Square, there were some cars and a motorbike waddling around the square, and Steve couldn't get into Whitehall. Instead, he went into Bridge Street and turned left onto the Embankment. If we'd taken Whitehall we'd have gone straight into an IRA mortar attack on Downing Street, which was happening at that very moment.

Over the years, other pieces of luck have resulted in us saving lives. Sir Peter Terry lived because his would-be assassin fired from too close range. Only chance stopped more death and destruction at the 1984 Tory Conference in

Brighton when the 'sleeper' bomb placed in Room 629 blew out the front of the Grand Hotel.

That assault on Downing Street was another. The Provisional IRA ASU had meticulously planned the mortar attack. They had worked out the trajectory and the exact place where their white van, acting as a missile launcher, had to be positioned.

It was at the junction with Whitehall. The van had a sticker on the windscreen that was behind the driver's mirror and lined up on a government building's flagpole. The calculation was a quarter-inch out. Right on target, they would have scored a direct hit on Number 10, where the then PM John Major was holding a Cabinet meeting.

We got Sir Charles back to Barclays HQ. But who knew what else might be going on? Where's the nearest safe house? Which routes are secure? What's the next appointment?

All the protection teams rang into the Yard to say where they were, if they were safe or if they needed any extra backup, more armed officers. We were ordered to get Sir Charles back to Hampshire.

I was 'guesting' with Sir Charles in July 1991, when, while awaiting trial, Pearse McAuley, who inexplicably had a semiautomatic pistol, and Nessan Quinlan escaped from Brixton Prison's high-security wing. Publicly, Sir Charles declared himself unconcerned by the escape and 'perfectly well looked after'.

I was with Sir Charles when news of the escape was announced. He was more than concerned: he was incandescent with rage. The Home Secretary was Kenneth Baker. Teflon Ken survived the situation, much to the annoyance of Sir Charles Tidbury.

I had already learned to be diplomatic, giving nods, not comments. What I hadn't been taught was evasive and close-protection driving skills. I was in the main SB office on the eighteenth floor of the Yard when that changed – I was going to the Gene Hunt School of Motoring (and anyone who's seen Life on Mars and Ashes to Ashes will know what I mean). I was to be taught security services 'defensive driving', including the formidable 180-degree 'J-turn' in reverse at speed.

There was a throwaway line from Dean, the transport manager: 'Next week, you're on your anti-hijack course at Hendon.'

Hendon Driving School is so renowned that coppers and spooks from all over the world use it. I arrived to be greeted by two other Special Branch guys, Sam and Richard. The rest of the course was made up of two royal chauffeurs and two royal backup drivers, which announced some fierce rivalry before we got started at Radlett airfield.

The place was deserted and the main runway was going to be used for the training. The complete runway would be used at first, made smaller with the use of cones until eventually we'd be doing high-speed turns in the width of a normal road.

John was one of the Queen Mother's chauffeurs. From my days in the Special Escort Group, I knew that she liked to sit with only one cheek on the seat, or sidesaddle. This was not the safest way to travel, as it was pointed out to her on numerous occasions, but she insisted on sitting this way. John told me that on more than one occasion she had slipped off the seat and onto the floor when he had to brake firmly or turn a corner.

There was to be lots of severe braking and accelerating in the next few days to learn to complete high-speed turns in the width of a normal road. First off was the J-turn. The principle was this: reverse for all your worth until you reach 30 m.p.h. – not something that you do down your local high street.

Then, with your right hand, pull the steering wheel down very hard and quick and, immediately that's completed, turn the wheel in the opposite direction as the car is spinning. In the middle of this, you have to switch from reverse to drive – the car is facing the correct way and you need to drive away under control but fast.

Next it was Y-turns, again reversing at speed but not as fast as the J-turn, turning the steering wheel violently but slamming on the brakes and making the car skid and turn around. This tactic is for narrow streets with little room to manoeuvre or turn.

Every moment was aimed at getting us to perfect the timing and coordination, and over the week the obstacle course was made ever more elaborate with a few extras. If reversing, a blanket was placed over the rear window, simulating shattered glass; another exercise involved a blanket over the windscreen. We'd lean out of windows while driving, shoot water pistols, throw water over 'attackers'.

It would make a marvellous turn on the TV programme *Top Gear*, as would ramming. This exercise involved four wrecked cars, which were just able to be driven. The art of ramming your way out of a road block is based on physics. We were told that we must aim to the rear of the blocking car. This way the engine would act as a fulcrum and the lighter rear end of the car would spin around that heavier front end.

We were kitted out in flameproof overalls, crash helmets, goggles and gloves. The college in-house fire officers were also on the scene just in case something went drastically wrong.

Once we had identified the road block and how the vehicles were positioned, we were told to stop the car, select first gear and accelerate hard, remaining in first. If you changed gears for that split second the car would slow down slightly – something that you didn't want. The knack is to aim for the rear of the blocking car and keep accelerating through that car.

We all had to start from the skidpan area and couldn't see how the vehicles were being positioned. I was driving an old Austin Allegro, a car that needed to be scrapped as soon as it came off the production line.

Driving high-performance cars to emergencies, fatal accidents, bank robberies, fights, the occasional riot, I'd never had an accident. Now I was going to create a big one. I felt a little mad; it was a Jeremy Clarkson moment. I adjusted my goggles, which by now were beginning to steam up, and floored the accelerator. I kept my foot rooted to the pedal, aiming to the rear of my target car. As I shot towards it, I braced myself for the impact. The engine was screaming at me as I slammed into the blocking cars. True to form, it spun out of the way on the axis of its own engine.

Keeping up the speed, I crashed the car into the road block with a resounding bang of metal colliding and that terrifying sound of glass shattering. My car slowed slightly on impact but, with my right foot glued to the floor, I powered my way through the cars and out the other end. I blew a huge sigh of relief, knowing that the physics worked.

I could drive evasively, I could shoot, but I'd still not been trained in the elaborate skills of close protection. Yet that was what I was employed to do in an often secret and always sinister world. There was no mention of doing the National

Bodyguard course. Special Branch were just too busy. They needed every man. In just one county, Wiltshire, there were four prominent IRA targets and protecting them was costing £1.5 million a year.

It was hard grind, but I loved it. One job to another, a few hours' sleep, up at 6 a.m. to drive back to the Yard bright-eyed and bushy tailed for a full day's work. This might have entailed driving in and all around London – or to Scotland. On four hours' sleep we carried guns and made life-or-death decisions and gave it not a thought; those long hours, at least a hundred hours of overtime a month, were not unusual.

At the Yard I was on the list of relieving SB detectives and drivers who fill in on the teams when people are on holiday, sick or doing refresher firearms courses. It could be disruptive with late-night callouts but I was happy with it as I met more and more officers and senior political figures. I was learning every day on the job. That was how it worked – you found out how to react by experience, not training.

I was in the main squad office shuffling paper, writing reports and filling in forms when my life changed. I remember all the details. I'd bought a sandwich, a chicken-and-avocado on brown, and a large coffee from Gino's, a café near the Yard, when my colleagues said I was needed urgently on the eighteenth floor.

I was met by one of the senior officers and we went to the superintendent's office. He said, 'Ah, there you are. Sit down. Can you go undercover for a while, for, say, about two weeks away from home? I need you to go now if you can.'

'I can, but what's the job?'

I was a little bemused by the abruptness of the request.

'Salman Rushdie,' he replied.

Holy shit!

Half the world wanted Rushdie – and anyone near him – dead.

I muttered, 'OK.'

The superintendent told me to go home and pack a bag for about two weeks. No suits, ties, very casual. Jeans, anything like that would be good. He told me, 'When you get back, one of the team members will collect you. Most important of all, don't tell anyone what you're doing. Is that clear?'

I looked at the two of them and said, 'Are you sure you've got the right man? You haven't got me mixed up with anybody else?'

The super smiled: 'No,' he said. 'You're just the chap.'

Again, I looked at them, waiting for the punchline, but nothing more was said.

I realised this must be for real.

Chapter Five
The Spectre
of Death

'I get up in the morning, spend the day working, and watch a lot of bad television. That's about it, except that I have a number of guests around. People with guns.'

Salman Rushdie, 1990

I only ever got to page 32 of Salman Rushdie's *The Satanic Verses* but find it truly ironic that two of the British institutions harshly treated in the novel, Margaret Thatcher and the police, became responsible for protecting the author's life.

Rushdie, who will always be known as 'Scruffy' to me and many of his Special Branch minders, has a way of ticking people off. Even his friends. Yet, even by his standards, he pulled off a monumental coup when Muslim critics called his book a criminally blasphemous insult to the Islamic faith and to the prophet Mohammed.

It began on 26 September 1988, when Viking Penguin published the book in the UK. Scruffy was accused of retelling sacred Islamic history with extravagant splashes of sex and fantasy. Nine days later, India banned the book, and Pakistan, Egypt, Saudi Arabia and South Africa did the same. In the following January the book was burned in Bradford, and on 12 February 1989 six people were killed in anti-Rushdie rioting in Islamabad; the next day one person was killed and more than a hundred were injured in the Indian part of Kashmir.

On 14 February – St Valentine's Day – Ayatollah Ruhollah Khomeini went on radio in Iran and pronounced, 'I inform the proud Muslim people of the world that the author of The Satanic Verses, which is against Islam and the prophet of the Koran, and all involved in its publication are sentenced to death.'

Within twenty-four hours the Iranians had put a $3 million dollar bounty on Scruffy's head. He'd hardly gone into hiding with his second wife, the writer Marianne Wiggins, when the kill fee was upped to $5.2 million dollars.

The fatwa – an Islamic ruling on a point of law, but, in Scruffy's case, a death sentence – was in place, and so, by then, was a Special Branch security shield. The fury against Salman Rushdie increased around the world by the day. Khomeini died that summer but that gave no reprieve – the death sentence was reissued. Bookshops in California were firebombed, hit squads wiped out the Japanese translator of The Satanic Verses and wounded the Norwegian publisher and Italian translator. By early 1990, Muslim leaders in the UK were demanding the book be withdrawn or they would 'pursue' their mission to kill.

When I began looking after him he was the Most Wanted Man Alive. A Squad were fair game – killing one of us would give them a nice cool $1 million. This was high-profile. I'd been in the department for only a short time and I'd been selected for one of the most dangerous jobs the Branch close-protection unit had ever done.

If we were found, our attackers had no problems dying for

their cause to avenge Allah. To say I was nervous and apprehensive that first day would be a gross understatement.

As instructed, I packed jeans, casual shirts, golf shirts, anything that didn't mark me out as a plainclothes policeman, and a few books and a Walkman. I put all this into a large holdall and returned to Scotland Yard.

Bob, a sergeant, introduced himself and said, 'Let's go.'

I picked up my holdall, which now also contained my Smith & Wesson and eighteen rounds of ammunition, and we went into the basement and found an old green Rover 216. I put my luggage on the back seat and got into the driver's seat. Bob got in next to me with a big smile and said, 'Do you know where you're going?'

'No.'

'I'll tell you the way.'

I looked at Bob. 'I realise that if you tell me you'll have to shoot me, but I'll take my chances.'

It broke the tension. Bob laughed and gave me directions to an address in Wimbledon Village. It was on a quiet road filled with very large Victorian houses. Most of them had huge windows and in-and-out gravel drives.

The property had double-fronted bay windows; the garage was on the left side and the doors were broken. Inside, it was big and imposing. The ground floor had three large reception rooms, and a large kitchen/diner. On the first and second floors were the bedrooms and more bathrooms.

Bob took me into one bedroom and said this was mine. It had a single bed and a shower in the corner. It overlooked the rear garden, which was slightly overgrown. Another officer, Keith, was cutting the grass. Bob joined me at the window, looked out and said:

'Not much else to do except to stay alive and cut the grass.'

It was the first time I had seen a gardener wearing a gun in a shoulder holster.

The houses surrounding us were of a similar size. The upper floors had a good view into 'our' rear garden. I was concerned that five men living in the same house might be the cause of some curiosity.

I unpacked and went downstairs into the front room. The rest of the team were watching daytime TV. I had met some of them before when they had 'guested' on teams I was on. The deal with Scruffy was that you lived with him for two weeks, went elsewhere for four weeks and then back.

Bob said, 'Let's go in and see the great man.'

'What's he like?'

'Well, he doesn't like the police, hates Thatcher, who stood up for him with a passion. He can be arrogant, and he's a socialist. Apart from that, he's all right.'

Bob knocked on the door and a soft, well-spoken voice answered. We walked in and he was sitting in a chair, reading. The room was big and very untidy. Papers and books were strewn everywhere around the desk and armchair. Heavy net curtains hung over the patio windows.

I knew Scruffy was a big-time writer and personality even before the ayatollah turned The Satanic Verses into a global bestseller, so the man himself was a surprise.

He was somewhat unkempt. He looked like Deputy Dawg peering through round glasses; he had tousled hair and clothes that just hung on him, creased. The blue shirt was wrinkled and he wore it over mangled tracksuit bottoms.

He'd won the Booker Prize in 1981 for *Midnight's Children* and numbered among his friends Melvyn Bragg, Martin

Amis, Ian McEwan, Fay Weldon and Harold Pinter and his wife, Lady Antonia Fraser. I was told he even had his own groupies. And this was the now even more famous, and infamous, author at home.

Bob introduced me and he stood up and gave me a handshake like a wet fish. My first impression was that of someone who was tolerant of me and no more.

We went back into the front room and Bob sat me down and said, 'The first thing you have got to do, to get into your brain straightaway, is not to call him Salman. His name is Joe. That's his cover name. He has a false passport to match his new identity. He's not allowed out or to have any friends around to visit. Not even his son.

'He's totally under arrest here, if that's the right term – a prisoner, under house arrest. Any callers are to be treated as a serious threat and all precautions taken. He won't have any visitors. No one knows we're here, not even the local police. The only people who know of our location are the senior management at Scotland Yard.

'However, there is a plan for extraction, under lock and key somewhere. I've not been told the location but the instructions are wrapped in a sealed envelope. I think it'll be with a superintendent at the local station. It is not to be opened unless we're all dead.

'But on to the important stuff. We do all our own cleaning, ironing, cooking, shopping and the rest. When we go to do our shopping, we generally ask Joe if he needs anything. We make a list of what we want, and he will give us his list. He eats crap anyway. He'll drink Michelob beers or Budweiser. He's also into crisps and other rubbish comfort food. When you go out shopping for him, don't give him the receipt.

'He has no idea how much things cost, so just round things up, if you know what I mean. At the end of two weeks, go and see him, tell him what he owes you. Just keep a running total of the stuff you bought for him and give him a round ballpark figure. Don't leave yourself short. He'll pay you in cash.

'Now, expenses. You will be here for two weeks. This weekend you should be off but the job will pay you red time [time and a half] and sixteen hours a day. We also get seventeen pounds a day meal expenses on top of that.

'We give Joe ten pounds a night lodging allowance, but we can claim twenty-five quid back from the job as a lodging allowance. When you pay for your accommodation, you're paying him in cash and he'll give you a receipt signed in his own fair hand. So we all get about thirty pounds a day, every twenty-four hours, plus overtime. The expenses are cash in hand, nontaxable in your back pocket. That's the vital stuff. Apart from that, there's not much else to tell you. Any questions?'

I shook my head which was about to explode. We were paying – or, rather, the taxpayer was paying – Rushdie to protect him! He was getting at least forty quid a night for the Special Branch to risk their lives to stop him being taken out by followers of the fatwa. And the government was providing the safe house!

Goodness, gracious, me!

I did have some questions, but I asked only those pertinent to protecting Joe. Who owned the house? Who came to the door? The postman or newspaper boys? Bob had the answers.

'All his mail is delivered to a false company, set up by the Met. It goes all around the houses but ends up in the Yard. Each day one of us will collect it. Only one team member is allowed out at any time. The house is rented from a female landlord but be careful, because she calls on the pretence of looking after her investment.

'Don't let her in under any circumstances. She's been told that this is a major police drug operation. We don't think she believes the story and keeps calling.

'The next thing you are going to know is that Joe has a friend, Elizabeth West. She's here most evenings. She's a proofreader for one of the publishing houses. You have to collect her from either the station or the Underground. She's been told to vary her route.

'When you collect her you take her for a drive to make sure she hasn't been followed. Be careful for it might be MI5 – they're watching her.'

So, spooks and possible hit squads on the streets of leafy Wimbledon. What would the neighbours think? For me, one of the most important things would be getting on with everybody in this claustrophobic experience. I guess it was like being in the Big Brother house. After a few days of being with the same people 24/7, small things can blow out of all proportion.

I prided myself that, having been in the department for only a very short time, I was picked. Obviously, my attitude over the previous months had been noticed, and not only by the guys I was now working with (for they must have said something to the senior management about whom they wanted).

Any group of people put together with the knowledge that there were people who were trying to kill them – Joe and them – and were willing to die in the process makes you work as a team and look after one another.

Keith told me, 'You've got the best room.'

'Your one must be crap, then.'

'No, it's OK, but you see that house with the blue curtains? Well, if you get up early enough, the bird in that room gets dressed with them open. She knows what she's doing and it starts the day off in the right way.'

I looked at him and we both smiled. Things were beginning to improve. This had the ingredients of a good team. Bob interrupted the daydreaming: 'Can you pick up Elizabeth?'

'What does she look like?'

'She's tall, about five eight, long black hair, and she has a Jewish look.'

Ah, great. That's all we need. Someone who has the Ayatollah Khomeini's death wish on his back and has a Jewish-looking girlfriend. Things could only get better really, couldn't they?

'She'll be wearing a long black coat with a long green scarf. She'll meet you at Southfields Underground station. Do the usual, pick her up, go for a drive and do a little dry cleaning.' ('Dry cleaning' meant checking to ensure we were not being tailed.)

The route to the station from the house was easy, but I decided to take a longer journey. The rush-hour traffic made it very difficult to determine whether you were being followed. What's that motorbike doing? He's travelling slow. What about that van? Or the blue Volvo? To find out if you're being followed you have to drive a little differently. Drive a little more slowly, or, when you can, faster.

At the Underground I bought a London *Evening Standard*, opened it to the property section and started looking at accommodation for the area. I had a pen in my hand, and was happily scoring out – I don't know what I was scoring out – when Elizabeth arrived.

I went up to her, held out my hand and said, 'Hi Elizabeth, I'm Ron.' I pointed to the property section in the paper, just in case anyone was looking, opened the car door, got in and we drove off.

I checked whether we were being tailed. The spooks had checked her out and she had no other family, the perfect plant. However, she seemed very pleasant with a soft voice and a lovely clear complexion. I wondered what first attracted her to the millionaire Salman Rushdie.

I tried to engage Elizabeth in small talk, trying to create an air of trust. She seemed to be on a different planet. She had a couple of plastic bags with her and Joe's evening meal, but one of our team had been out shopping and Joe was already into the beer and crisps.

We settled down in another room and were discussing the rights and wrongs between Christianity and the Muslim faith when Bob walked in with four glasses of red wine. I was settling into this Special Branch way of life, and putting my conscience neatly to one side, readily accepted Bob's offering. I said it was amazing how you could turn water into wine in this department. I was reliably informed that this was a valuable trick passed down by many Special Branch officers over the years, and was a tradition that kept on flowing.

Of course, they were different days. Muslim fundamentalists and Osama bin Laden were some way off, and so were the Arab countries that were pushing extremism, and the abandonment of the freedom that we take for granted. These were the atrocities that would come to haunt us, putting new meaning into the role of A Squad.

When I was guarding Joe, the protection was basic. I hadn't even completed the National Bodyguard Course, but here I was protecting a very high-profile person with little or no relevant training. Suicide bombers were not even planned for. This kind of extreme action took place only in the Middle East, not Middle England. To protect Joe and ourselves, all we had were our Smith & Wessons and eighteen rounds each. We were not trained to carry carbines, and, because of internal politics, the turf wars in the Met Police, only SO19 (firearms branch) officers were carbine-trained and they would not train us. If we needed heavyweight weapons, SO19 officers were attached to them, and that wouldn't happen.

When I look back at how little we were prepared for our task, I realise we were placed in a very dangerous position. If a similar protection came about in 2008, it would be done completely differently.

Certainly, at least, without the wine. We'd had a couple of bottles of red and were looking for more. On the floor behind me were about a dozen bottles of France's finest. Just by looking at the labels you could tell it was good stuff. I picked one up and said, 'Let's open this one and we can replace it.'

Bob said, 'Hang on a minute, I'll go and ask Joe if we can buy it.'

That seemed a better idea, so Bob went off to ask Joe. A minute later he returned saying, 'Yep, that's OK.'

I eagerly picked up the bottles and inspected the labels. Bob added, 'Joe says it'll cost us forty-five quid a bottle.'

Joe wanted corkage! It was too heavy a price to pay. Our thirst was somewhat quenched by that news, and I gently replaced the bottle. Joe was clearly not a generous man. Bob's words about Joe's not liking the police, especially those risking their lives for him, echoed. The mood had changed.

I washed up the cutlery and took a look through the

Above: Hello, hello, hello! Carefree days as a young copper fooling around on Derby Day at Epsom in 1981.

Below: Another Derby Day mugshot.

Above: Happy days – on traffic patrol in Trafalgar Square.

Below: A Glock handgun of the type I frequently carried on duty as a protection officer.

Above: 'Helmet and Safety' – they didn't want us to hurt ourselves during close
encounters of the motor vehicle kind.

Below: Making like Gene Hunt on an anti-hijack course.

Above: Bullseye! That's me hitting the targets smack on.

Below: The result of my crash, bang, wallop!

Above: I'll take the high road – on duty with an off-duty Home Secretary Kenneth Baker on Rannoch Moor.

Below: Ready to spin the Range Rover wheels.

The boys in blue – on the Tory campaign trail with Baker.

Above: Not the sort of briefing we were used to at Scotland Yard – instructions before beating for Tom King's shoot.

Below: On the beat on King's farm for a pheasant shoot.

Above: Tom King (in glasses) with hot toddy in hand during a day's shooting. Special Branch did the honours that day, handing out the hot drinks.

Below: Birds for the pot – the haul of pheasants from Tom King's estate.

kitchen cupboards. Keith came in. 'For goodness' sake, don't take any of his food,' he said. 'He goes mad if you do.'

Bedtime. Bob said he would check that the alarms were working. The entire perimeter of the house was fitted with covert infrared beams, which were sometimes triggered by the moon, tree branches, a cat or fox, but you never knew who might be out there, so we all slept with our guns within easy reach.

We all used to be up and dressed by 8 a.m. and have breakfast together of Sugar Puffs or Rice Krispies followed by toast and coffee while walking around the house wearing our guns. It was a bright sunny morning when there was a knock on the front door and that set off our mental alarms: there was no need for anyone to knock on the door; all the bills were paid direct, the post was redirected by the Yard's front company, and we had no milk or newspaper deliveries.

The front door had a big glass panel and through it we could see a small figure of an Indian or Arab-looking boy. One of the team, a gun nut called Phil, immediately went into overdrive, drawing his revolver, ready to kill the boy on the front step.

I shouted, 'Hang on, it's only a kid!'

Phil was having none of it. As far as he was concerned, this was going to be a hit. They had found us and were going to kill us all. Scruffy was alerted and frogmarched up the stairs and into his room overlooking the rear garden The rest of the team were poised, weapons drawn, behind walls in the house and ready to start shooting. It was getting very tense, no thanks to Phil, who by this time was in the aim position ready to kill the kid on the doorstep.

I thought, 'What the fuck's going on?' And I shouted

out, 'Someone has to go to open the door and find out what he wants.'

Phil said, 'It's an Arab kid and could be hostile. It could be a setup.'

I told him, 'If it is, we're all dead. Someone has to find out first.'

The doorbell rang again. Phil was ready for anything now. We all had our guns out and were ready to take on the threat. One of the team was a female officer called Laura. She said that she would answer the door and find out what he wanted.

She put her gun in the small of her back inside the belt of her trousers, and made her way to the front door. The rest of the team were up in the aim position, with Phil ready for war. I was in the aim, too, pointing straight at the kid. I was standing at the bottom of the stairs, and just behind me, a couple of steps up, was Keith.

If the shit did hit the fan he would run up the stairs to where Scruffy was hiding and try to protect him for as long as he could until help arrived. It had better come quickly – we could do our eighteen rounds in seconds, and that would be that.

Laura opened the door with her hand behind her back holding her gun, ready to pull it out and use it. The rest of us braced ourselves, aiming down the hall.

'I've come to collect the paper money.'

Laura told him we didn't have papers delivered. The boy looked at the number of the house and said, 'Sorry, miss, I've come to the wrong house.'

He turned and walked back up the drive. Laura closed the door and walked back down the hall. We all relaxed and put our weapons back into our holsters – apart from Phil, who took a few more seconds to do the same and said, 'That was a close call.'

I was furious. 'Who for? Us or the fucking kid you almost killed?'

He then tried to justify his actions. I had some sympathy and understanding of what he was saying, but he went straight to killing mode. If we were going to be in trouble, the last person I wanted to be standing next to was Phil. We all calmed down and smoothed over the tensions between us. Living under these conditions put an untold strain on all of us. We had to be a team and work as a team. The whole thing would fall apart if we didn't pull together, and this highlighted the enormous strain that we were all under doing this job under 'house arrest'.

Now, with the years of experience and the deity of hindsight, it amazes me what I was doing without proper training.

If things had gone wrong I was supposed to fire my gun – with another officer in the way blocking me – and hit the kid. I hadn't been trained as a sharpshooter. Even if I had I doubt I could have pulled that shot off without killing some of the wrong people. What would have happened if I had made a fatal mistake and killed someone and it came out in the inquest that my training was not to a suitable standards? The thought makes me sweat now.

Back then I didn't think about it, but it was stupid to send a guy into a situation like that without giving him the proper training. It wouldn't be the last time that happened either.

Keith brought Scruffy downstairs. He was a little shaken, just like the rest of us, but we kept it all hidden from him. He had to trust us. I knew that an important aspect of protection work is to build a rapport with your principal, otherwise it makes the tolerable pretty much intolerable, especially when you are living with the target.

A story from the early days of the fatwa was that the original team with him got so fed up with Scruffy's attitude and antics that they locked him in a cupboard under the stairs and all went to the local pub for a pint or two. They came back, suitably refreshed, and let him out.

Until then, my perception of Joe was one that I had been given by the rest of the team. One day he made himself a cup of coffee and joined us, sitting next to me at the kitchen table. We had a lively discussion about politics and I realised how much he hated the Tories, and Margaret Thatcher in particular. He really did let rip over Maggie, albeit that she'd stood up for him and his work and the threats from Tehran, defending freedom of speech and the rights of others.

Joe wanted a socialist government and Neil Kinnock was their man, but, as far as I was concerned, whatever side of the fence you were standing on, a dyslexic monkey would have been better than Kinnock. That didn't seem to get much airtime with Joe but the two of us tried to get a relationship going.

After our chats Joe would go back upstairs and continue his writing. Part of that, which we didn't know about, was an ongoing, detailed log of his Special Branch protection, our names, our routine and tactics.

I'd been on duty in Wimbledon for a couple of months on and off when the shit hit the fan. We'd been compromised – the death squads out to get Scruffy knew where we were.

It was lunchtime when the top brass, the head of E Squad, which watches Islamic extremists, and our boss from A Squad, arrived at the house. We had to get out. Now!

Scruffy was shitting himself and, to be fair, so were we. We had no idea how the bad guys had found us. The major problem was that the Yard department that deals with safe houses couldn't get us anything suitable quickly. The longer we hung around, the more deadly the situation.

Scruffy rang around his friends. The prolific poet James Fenton stood up for him. He said we could use his cottage in Cumnor in Oxfordshire. It was panic stations from that moment. We had to pack up everything, including Scruffy, and make sure no clues to our possible whereabouts were left. Bags and bags of paperwork were burned in the fireplace, perimeters checked, the whole surrounding area monitored, and secure transport and routes organised.

We arrived at the cottage at 3 a.m. and Fenton welcomed us with tea and biscuits. Then, wisely, he and his Chinese friend left us to it.

The world was full of furious Muslims and here we were in the middle of the English countryside waiting for them to descend.

Chapter Six
Killing Me Softly

'In the city you get the problem of houses being close together. In the countryside, the problem is people are nosey. It requires a great deal of skill. I might be living next door to you and you would never know it.'

Salman Rushdie, August, 1998

It was scary. We had to make this new countryside environment secure as fast as possible but without alerting the locals. The cottage was smaller than the property in Denmark Hill, with room for only two SB officers to stay on camp beds overnight. I and another officer, Ray, found a local bed-and-breakfast, but it was risky.

The owner of the B&B was inquisitive. Had we had a good day? Where had we been? What did we do? Ray and I had already discussed our cover story. Ray wanted to be a tax inspector. I wasn't keen on that one. Anyway, what would two taxmen be doing out here?

We decided on working for the BBC looking for locations for future TV shows. Our host would not stop asking questions. What shows? Period? Comedy?

The next morning our nightmare came in with two full English breakfasts and said, 'I've been thinking about what you were saying last night and about locations. Have you seen this?'

He opened the curtains in grand style. I nearly choked. The cottage next door was straight off a postcard. Thatched roof, eighteenth-century, authentic-looking windows and doors, finished off with whitewashed walls. Lovely location. We babbled some story about a tight schedule and returning, but we never did.

Things had calmed down at the cottage. I went over to James Fenton's CD collection and had a look through. I chose the best of Roberta Flack and put it on. I didn't realise it would make Scruffy romantic. He wanted to give Elizabeth some fun and he wanted privacy. Bob was explaining this and I said that having us around hadn't put Scruffy off his stroke in the past.

Yet, it was decided that, once our meal had finished, the two who were staying elsewhere would go and the other two must go to their rooms, solitary confinement. When we complained, it was pointed out that Joe was paying for the cottage, so he could request what he liked. Being locked up all evening and having to listen to Scruffy doing horizontal press-ups with Elizabeth was beyond the call of duty. But there wasn't much we could do about it.

This two-week stint over, I was back at the Yard, but Scruffy was still on the agenda. My commander called me in. 'That place in Wimbledon – we've got to give it back. Can you and Laura go round, give it a clean and make sure that nothing's left behind? The owner's becoming a pest and we need to give it back to her as soon as possible.'

I was not really looking forward to this particular job. It's one thing to keep your own house tidy but to do it for Scruffy was something else. Laura called me into the dining room. Sitting in the middle of the table was one of those mock silver candelabra and over time the wax had melted onto the table, causing a miserable mess of hardened wax. I went into Scruffy's en suite. I've never seen such filth. I don't think anything had been cleaned all the time we were there.

When we reported back on the situation, the superintendent said that we weren't trained for such horror. He would get industrial cleaners in.

In the early days of Special Branch we were known as 'hush-hush men' because rarely did our role become public. It was difficult to live up to that name in the countryside. The Oxfordshire villagers were getting more and more curious about James Fenton's 'guests' and it was difficult to keep our distance, and Scruffy's identity, from them. We needed a new home.

The imposing house in Highgate was big enough to accommodate all of us. To the front were 12-foot-high black railings and an in-and-out drive. There was shrubbery behind these railings and this meant all movements from the front of the house were totally obscured. To the left was a double garage. Through the front door to the right was another reception room. French windows opened up onto a patio area, a wonderful garden and a spectacular heated pool that was at the bottom of the garden.

Before we arrived, we had been given a special brief about this tour of duty. We were told to keep our guns with us at all times, not because of the bad guys, of whom there were many, but because there was a feeling that Joe was getting suicidal. Psychologists warned us he might kill himself.

Police psychologists and other experts had been analysing

his situation and behaviour. I believe he always knew he was going to piss off a lot of people with The Satanic Verses, but the reaction was more than he ever imagined – and wasn't going away.

Originally, he'd been told the politicians would solve the problem and he would be under SB protection for a week at the most. Initially, he 'hid' in a hotel in the Cotswolds. The clock had ticked on.

He had been under virtual house arrest for almost a year and it was beginning to get to him. He'd rarely show up before 10.30 in the morning. He mumbled about the place. It was jail but without the rigorous routine of a penitentiary, which helps keep long-term prisoners sane. The last thing the Yard needed was for Joe to top himself by putting one of our guns to his head. With that foremost in our minds, we kept our revolvers attached to our belts at all times.

The evenings were always a problem with boredom. One of the guys joined the local video club and we'd watch a movie coupled with a bottle of wine and a few beers.

When I talked to Scruffy, it was clear that one of the toughest things for him, and understandably so, was not being able to see his son Zafar, by his first wife Clarissa Luard. Zafar would have been around ten years old then, not old enough to keep his father's location secret from his friends. Joe kept in touch by phone, but this separation was causing problems. And everyone involved was already concerned about his mental health.

The school Zafar was at knew of the boy's difficulties and there were special arrangements should there be any suspect enquiries about him. The fear was that, if father and son were seen together, the boy could be kidnapped and held for ransom in return for his father and thereby his father's life.

It was decided by Special Branch and the security services that a visit would be in order. One senior SB deskman had the bright idea of blindfolding Zafar and taking him to Hampstead; that was the level of thinking that was around at the time. It was ignored.

We got around the problem with a Sunday afternoon family outing: we would all go to Epping Forest and play cricket. I went to find a suitable location for our match and there was a good spot next to where cars could be parked in case we were compromised and had to make a quick getaway.

On the day, I went to the north London address where Zafar and his mother were living. I was looking out for good guys, bad guys or journalists. Senior officers thought that Scruffy, ever one for publicity, might have contacted a friendly newspaper for a photo opportunity.

As with all kids getting into a car with a strange man, it was a little frightening for him, but his mother was there and reassured him. Joe had spoken to him and told him what I looked like. We zipped along to a small street by Billingsgate Market where Elizabeth and Joe were waiting. It was an emotional meeting. They talked for fifteen minutes while the team watched every rooftop, every moment around them.

When we got to Epping there were lots of families enjoying the sunshine. We busied ourselves putting the stumps into the ground and getting our picnic ready. The whole team made the effort to make the time, the short time that Joe had with his son, memorable. We gave Zafar the bat and Joe prepared to bowl. I was wicketkeeper and the rest of the team took up any fielding positions they could think of. Some people watched us playing and a few nudged each other and pointed to Scruffy.

They would do a double-take and then dismiss it as impossible and move on. It was fun for us as well to get out of the house and to relax in this family atmosphere. During our cricket match, we had to be careful not to let anyone see our weapons.

All the running around was taking its toll on Scruffy's capacity to breathe. He hadn't been bowling for long when he placed his hands on his knees and was blowing hard. He couldn't even talk. I made sure that I moved away from him. I didn't fancy giving him mouth-to-mouth. Yet Joe was particularly animated about his afternoon in the sun with his son, even if he did almost require an oxygen tent!

The afternoon ended too soon for father and son. We drove off to a different changeover point; we never used the same place twice, just in case. The parting was as upsetting as the reunion had been uplifting. I had the job of taking Zafar home. The journey was quiet, with the little boy wondering what all the fuss was about and why he couldn't go to his dad's house. At his home, I checked the house out, made sure his mother was safe and got him indoors.

It was clear to me and the others that keeping Joe under lock and key was not sustainable. He must be allowed to visit friends and try to reintroduce himself into the wider world. Film premieres, literary events – these would place an even greater risk on all of us. One idea was some kind of disguise. Scruffy was scruffy. To counter his highly recognisable look he was to get a makeover. His image was to be sharpened up.

To cover up his baldness, he was going to be fitted for a wig. The team burst out laughing. We couldn't wait to see him fitted with a rug – and the astonishing thing was that he agreed to it. The last thing he had ever worried about was his appearance.

No one was allowed to come into the house, so he had to

go to the carpet fitter. Just off Highgate High Street there was a police section house, accommodation blocks for single officers. This was where Salman Rushdie would get the Hollywood treatment. Without the red carpet. He arrived in a long black coat with the collar up.

The wig maker had arrived earlier with a large bag containing the tools of his trade. The first thing he had to do was make a mould of Scruffy's dome. He delved into his box of tricks and pulled out a roll of clingfilm. After he had wrapped his head like a Christmas turkey, a solution was smeared all over. He sat there for about thirty minutes to let the solution set. He was not happy, especially when we kept giving him the thumbs-up, telling him it would be worth it.

Summer arrived and the SB team were making good use of the pool, which was thankfully heated. There was a games room and we often played table tennis. From time to time Joe joined in, and, as always, he fancied himself as a good player. On one occasion we started to play and I won. The gauntlet was thrown down and he wanted to play another game. Knowing him quite well by now, I felt it imperative that he didn't win. If he did, then he would attempt to rub it in and be a pain. If he lost, then he would get even more annoying, but we preferred him that way than in the winning mode. We played about nine games and I prevailed, much to his annoyance.

One evening by the pool, we were joined by Joe and Elizabeth. We were having a very enjoyable time, a few beers, and Joe was in sparkling form. He then suggested buying a barbecue. We all agreed that that would be a good idea. Albert – our own SB Del Boy – said he knew someone who could supply one at a knockdown price. As if! This was going to cost Scruffy.

The barbecue, a gas fire with all mod cons, arrived. Albert was given cash for it, a couple of hundred pounds over the odds. One of the guys went out to buy steaks and sausages and Joe said that he would pay for it all – but he had done, anyway. He just didn't know it.

Sitting in the garden of this marvellous house on a warm summer's evening, guzzling beers and telling stories, Joe loved the spotlight. He was very amusing and kept the party alive for many hours. The conversation centred on the world of books and writing. I mentioned that I enjoyed the work of John le Carré. Big mistake.

Le Carré had spoken out about the soft-cover publication of *The Satanic Verses* and Salman Rushdie's position and how it could put booksellers and publishing employees at risk. He said in the *New York Times* in 1989,

> I don't think it is given to any of us to be impertinent to great religions with impunity. I am mystified that he hasn't said, 'It's all a mess. My book has been wildly misunderstood, but as long as human lives are being wasted on account of it, I propose to withdraw it.' I have to say that would be my position.

He elaborated on this in a 1990 biography by W J Weatherby, saying,

> Again and again, it has been within his power to save the faces of his publishers and, with dignity, withdraw his book until a calmer time has come. It seems to me he has nothing more to prove than his own insensitivity.

Le Carré had also allegedly slagged off one of Joe's books and Joe was very vocal in returning the compliment.

With time, the situation was getting a little more relaxed. A number of invitations were arriving. All of them would have to be vetted to see if we could manage the security situation as well as not raising his profile too much and flaming the fatwa.

He was asked to appear on London Weekend Television's The South Bank Show, hosted by his pal Melvyn Bragg. The show was recorded in front of a live studio audience. I was picked to help with the security arrangements.

Joe was brought to the show early and taken to a dressing room to have make-up put on. All live TV shows go through a procedure of vetting studio audience for troublemakers, but not like this one. They were screened when they came in just in case one of the production team couldn't keep the news to themselves and there were unwanted guests arriving.

They were then herded together and brought into the studio. The security team manned all the exits. Melvyn Bragg came in and told the audience he had a very special guest and once the show started no one would be allowed to leave. If for some reason they had to go to the bathroom, someone would escort them there and back. They would not be allowed to leave the building while the show was being recorded.

The build-up went on for a few minutes and then our man entered the arena. The applause was polite and enthusiastic and Scruffy took a bow and they got on with it.

We returned to the Festival Theatre after some bright spark turned one of Joe's books, *Haroun and the Sea of Stories*, into a theatrical event. The cast were unaware he'd make regular visits, by bulletproof Jag, to rehearsals. It cost tens and tens of thousands of pounds in security. We needed manpower for there was no way we could keep him a secret once he arrived. A labyrinth of corridors and doors led onto other corridors, entrances and exits. Once my colleague Ben and I had completed our security assessment, we knew we could not put anything worthwhile in place because of the openness of the building and all the people coming and going.

It was one day, one moment, at a time. We would place a man outside all the doors with two of us inside the rehearsal room. The cars would be outside at the quickest exit and the drivers had to stay with the cars all day.

Ben and I guarded Joe from his headstrong attitude and watched the production develop. Each morning started with meditation and yoga. Joe decided to join in, telling the cast that he wanted to be at one with them and showing them that he wanted to take a full part in the production. During all of this, he had also decided that it would be a good idea if we were not in the room. Two cynical coppers looking at all this was stopping the positive energy that everyone was getting from these sessions. We watched over him through the glass window in the door.

The rehearsal room next door was also in use. The cast were there rehearsing *Antony and Cleopatra*, which the National Theatre was going to stage. I looked into that room and saw Alan Rickman and Helen Mirren. I watched the rehearsal with interest. It's serious work with fine actors. It was very interesting to see how this production came together.

Over the hours, I noticed that these two leading lights of the stage world hardly ever spoke to each other unless it was in the script. When Mirren was doing her bit, Rickman was reading the newspaper.

At lunch break in the canteen they didn't so much as look at each other. Yet they were the centre of attraction until Scruffy shuffled in. A gasp went around the room, again, as he waited in line for his food, all the heads turning one way, and then the other, looking for the heavies with the dark glasses and rippling muscles. We were just four guys scattered around the canteen eating sandwiches. I would look straight ahead but concentrate on what was going on at the edge of my vision.

The arrival and departure times were the most dangerous and we tried to vary them, but it was not always that easy. Joe would let us know when he wanted to leave. A few of the guys would make their way out onto the street and walk up and down looking into the cars as discreetly as possible, looking for any would-be assassin or journalists. It was always a security profile.

If you saw a middle-aged, white man in a suit, the probability was that he might not be one of the bad guys. If you saw an Asian aged between seventeen and forty, then it might be trouble. Some of the liberal human-rights groups may not like that, but I'm sorry, that was a fact of life for us.

It was becoming more relaxed at the house, even though the threat level was still very high. He was still not allowed to have friends to the safe house. We were told that he wanted to try to lobby the Labour Party and his friends within it to get the government to push his case harder with the Iranians and attempt to get the fatwa lifted.

His view was that the Foreign Office was not working hard enough on his behalf. All political links to Iran had been severed after the Iranian Embassy terrorist siege of 1980 (which had been ended by the SAS), and so any contact had to be done through another embassy.

This cut little ice with Scruffy. He wanted to have a series of meetings with senior Labour figures in an attempt to get John Major's Tory government to do more. He thought getting some Opposition heavyweight involved would put greater emphasis into his argument. The Labour MP for Leicester East, Keith Vaz, had said what an outrage the fatwa was. Scruffy enlisted his help

However, the more that Vaz talked about the fatwa, the more it became apparent that his stance was not endearing him to the vast majority of his mainly Muslim constituency. In a relatively short space of time the good people of Leicester East told Mr Vaz to shut up on the Rushdie issue or risk being deselected. Democracy in action!

MPs say anything to get elected but, once they're safely inside the House of Commons and see the benefits of keeping to the party line, they all fall into place. They don't want to be thrown off the huge gravy chain by doing something stupid like representing someone who may be killed. Keith Vaz quietly slipped beneath the surface and made no further statements on... Salman who?

Of course, Salman Rushdie deserved any help he could get. He set up meetings with anyone brave enough to raise their head above the parapet. He told Tony, the team leader, he had arranged a few dinners with his close circle of friends and gave him the dates.

They were sent on to A Squad command at the Yard and to the security services. We knew MI5 and MI6 would monitor us. They used it as some kind of training exercise.

On one occasion we spotted them and thought it would be a good idea to give them a runaround, which we did. There were cars and motorbikes dashing all over the place. The best way to find out if you are being followed is to go through a red traffic light to see if they have the nerve to follow. It livened things up.

Special Branch had only a few armoured Jags, and it wouldn't take long for any would-be assassin to work out which these were. The majority were owned and driven by the government car service. These drivers were civilians who drove senior government ministers, including at the time, the prime minister.

They were not entirely trained in the skills of driving, or even given the basic course in protection. We all knew that, if a government minister was attacked while being driven by one of these guys, then we were in big trouble. They were not authorised to carry firearms.

The superintendent in charge of our particular operation knew of someone who was selling an armoured BMW at a very reasonable cost. The case was put to Scruffy that, if he wanted to move around London covertly, then he ought to buy this vehicle. BMWs are to be seen all over the place. However, a black Jag always made people look and it was apparent to everyone that the car was armoured.

He bought the BMW. The annoying feature with this was the radio and CD player. Not much of a problem, but there was a little device whereby he could change channel and up the volume, all from the comfort of the rear seat. He loved the gadget. He would give anyone who got in the car the full tour of all this control did.

One evening, Scruffy told us he was going to have supper

with Channel 4's Jon Snow at the broadcaster's whitewashed home in a quiet cul-de-sac in Camden, north London. I went with one of the other guys to do a discreet reconnaissance of the house. We made a decision not to contact Snow or his family before the dinner so as not to worry them unduly.

No one other than the team knew the address we were going to. It was all very low-key – just how we and Scruffy all liked it. On the night, the door was answered by Snow himself, a very tall man, grey-haired and slimly built. He was casually dressed. After taking a look at our ID, he invited us in. The house was full of children, toys scattered all over the place. The smell of cooking was coming from the kitchen.

In one of the main reception rooms the other guests were waiting for Salman's arrival. They included Neil and Glenys Kinnock and Michael Foot. Kinnock was now the established leader of the Labour Party but on this occasion he was accompanied by his wife. They all said hello and allowed us to carry out our jobs without interference. We both looked all around the house, checking that they were not being held hostage until the main guest arrived.

His entire circle of friends had been warned that, if they invited him to their homes, or to other venues, then it would be in their best interests to keep that information on a need-to-know basis for everyone's safety, including their own.

Usually, the PPO will make sure that the area is safe for the principal to get out of the car, and open the door for him. However, in Scruffy's case, as this was a covert protection, and we tried to draw as little attention as possible to ourselves, we used to do the complete opposite.

The PPO would let him open his own door. The rest of the team would be scattered about the area to provide gun cover for the car. The doors were bulletproof and heavy and, if the car was on an incline, Scruffy would sometimes have to struggle to open the door. We used to help the poor old boy but, if he was being particularly difficult, we would let him struggle.

We got the call that he was only a few minutes away. I stood by the front door of the house keeping it slightly ajar for him to sweep in. As the evening rolled on, you could hear the talk coming around to what could be done for Salman. Michael Foot was very keen to do as much as he could. Everyone always does when there's nothing to lose. Neil Kinnock was a little more reticent and you could hear him come out with his usual of, 'I would like to do more but... '

We all looked at one another and thought the same old story: sell him a dream and then give him a nightmare; say one thing in the press but in reality there's not much anyone can do to help. After about four hours Rushdie gave us the nod and the backup team left the house to make sure the safe house had not been compromised.

My colleague at the time went up and checked Salman's study area and found some papers on his desk, which was nothing unusual, but something made him read them.

Later, with Scruffy secure, he told me that good old Salman was keeping a diary on all of us. He had dates and times, names and how much we had given him in rent, and it was all on paper. It was stunningly obvious that when all this was over he was going to write another book about his time under the fear of death and being protected by Met Police Special Branch. We were told that the details of the names and dates were spot on.

It infuriated me – here we were protecting him and he was

making notes which also might make money if published, but that wasn't the time for him even to attempt to publish. He remained assessed at what's known as threat level 2. The threat levels went from 5 up to 1. The security services and Special Branch always tried to avoid putting people at threat level 1 because it unnerved everyone and the cost spiralled.

There was already a political storm about the protection being afforded to Scruffy. Personal detectives had been withdrawn from many public figures, politicians and judges who were under IRA threat. The twenty-four-hour guard on Scruffy was a significant factor in the budget cutbacks; the cost in manpower and overtime meant others had to go it alone.

Salman Rushdie was headlines. Yet, even when he was at most risk, he went up to threat level 1 for only a short time and then back down to 2, alongside Margaret Thatcher. An odd couple – with assassination squads their only link (and, of course, Margaret Thatcher was under threat from the Provisional IRA and not from Islamic extremists).

At level 2, however, it was still thought a good idea to let Scruffy out to visit his friends, otherwise we could all go stir crazy. We started to go out. We would be told a few days prior to the event whom we were going to see and what the function was. It was generally a dinner or small party with a pal, such as Martin Amis or Mariella Frostrup. One of the better occasions was an evening at Marie Helvin's flat in west London. She was one of the original supermodels and once the wife of the photographer David Bailey. When we arrived with Scruffy, he went into the main room while she waltzed us into her bedroom, which had a large TV screen at the end of the bed.

With a naughty smile she said the regular films were by the TV and the sexier films were in the drawer. I did try one or two of the more adult films. Scruffy knew what had gone on, and on the journey home piled on the comments. He'd had a few drinks and let what he had of his hair down.

The evening had gone well, the mood created by the host.

On another evening we went to the architect Richard Rogers's beautiful period house just off the Kings Road. Our man went off to be entertained and while their maid took us to the back stairs where we were escorted out onto the roof garden. This was the best one yet. We were slightly bemused why we ended up out in the cold. We'd all brought jackets, which hid our weapons, so it wasn't that bad, but it wasn't very comfortable, either.

I can't remember how long we were in the enchanted garden, but when the novelty wears off and you start getting cold and hungry it's long enough. We weren't even given a drink – and his wife Ruth Rogers is a co-owner of the rather well-known River Café! Our time there would have paid for a cup of tea, even at her prices.

When it was time to go we went downstairs with our collars up and blowing into our hands; this had no effect on anybody but it made us feel better.

Security assessments were constantly made on Zafar Rushdie, who was obviously getting older and more aware of the threat against his father. The lack of contact between them was still causing some angst, but the lad was still under the threat of kidnapping and contact still had to be made under our control. At one stage the idea of placing the son under constant guard was still a very real option, but not implemented.

Yet, understandably, father wanted to see son. I was

detailed to pick up Zafar from his North London school and bring him to a neutral venue. It was arranged that I would meet him outside the main gates at the school at 4 p.m. The school bell sounded and the school exit was suddenly a mass excitement of parents and children looking for one another. I was no exception. I was looking for one particular schoolboy as well as any potential danger.

The rush of kids coming out of the school was beginning to slow and at 4.20 p.m. I was quite concerned. Most of the other kids in the cars had gone. I walked up and down the road looking along the high street, but didn't see anyone waiting.

The headmaster knew of this one extra-special pupil, and I went into the school to try to find him and enquire if anything was wrong. A teacher told me that Zafar's class had swimming lessons in the afternoon but the coach had returned and everyone was gone. I asked if they were absolutely sure that everyone was back. I was told that, yes, the pupils were back.

But one was missing. I didn't want to push the panic button too soon until I had gone through all my options at the school, but I didn't have any options.

My mobile rang. It was the team with Scruffy asking where we were and was everything OK? I said that there may be one slight problem and I would call them back in a few minutes, and that there was nothing to worry about. I had to stall them for a few minutes until I was absolutely sure of my facts and circumstances. I felt bad not telling the team the real reason, but something was bound to show on their faces and panic Scruffy. I didn't wish that on him.

Time was slipping by and the situation was becoming more desperate by the minute. I was getting to the stage where I couldn't stall any longer, and I would have to call the office and tell them that somebody had got the boy.

My mobile went again and as calmly as I could I spoke to Dan, the team leader. 'Keep him happy,' I said, 'but the son's gone missing and no one can find him. Give me a few more minutes and I'll call you to let you know what's happening.'

If he had been kidnapped, any further delay would cause the trail to get cold; the likelihood of catching the kidnappers was being reduced by the minute. I had to tell the office and raise the alarm.

I started to dial the Yard when the headmaster came over and, in a very casual manner, said, 'I just heard from the games master. Two buses were laid on today and the second was delayed and will be here in a few minutes. Master Rushdie is safely on it.'

I asked him to confirm that Zafar was actually on the bus. He nodded to the bus, which was arriving at the school gates, and off jumped my passenger. He was blissfully unaware of the sheer, blind panic that had been caused.

Salman Rushdie began to go out to more public events. He was instantly recognisable wherever he went, which caused all sorts of problems. The main criteria now when he was invited to these events was that there be no advance publicity.

Our tactics changed as well. We had to operate in a discreet manner which allowed us to remain hidden to any observers.

The overt team were allocated a small office on the sixteenth floor of Scotland Yard and Rushdie's engagements were still kept to a need-to-know basis. The access to this office was strictly for the team members only. The tactical change brought about other problems that had to be solved.

The more Scruffy attended public events, the more danger it caused from Islamic terrorists and annoyance from the press eager to catch us out and locate the safe house.

Scruffy started to stay out later and later, enjoying his newfound freedom. It became very tiring for the teams and the cost was rocketing all the time – without doubt the most expensive protection operation ever mounted or maintained. And we were earning a fortune.

So presumably was Salman Rushdie. People wanted to read about his notoriety. He couldn't write books or articles fast enough. He was friendly with Andreas Whittam Smith, co-founder and then editor of the Independent, and they published articles he bashed out. Presumably, having a contributor who was under threat of death added some frisson to the editorial pages. It certainly didn't thrill us, for it kept Scruffy's face and profile in the spotlight and the fatwa in the headlines.

The protection team looking after Salman Rushdie didn't change much over the years. It was essential that there be little movement of personnel. The fewer people who know about an operation, the less chance of security breaches.

Around the end of my term with Scruffy, the Metropolitan Police got another shock about the cost of his protection. Stephen, who had been on the team from the start, was about to retire. He had lived with Salman Rushdie for two-week periods and got paid for sixteen hours a day. He reckoned he was due more money, as he'd worked twenty-four-hour days.

He submitted a bill for twenty-four hours through his solicitor and it landed on Commissioner Paul Condon's desk. The commissioner, after choking on his morning coffee, decided to fight the claim. However, one by one, other officers who were on the team for a number of years, and also about to retire, submitted similar claims. The Met had a financial fight on its hands over Rushdie. And, surprisingly, no word of this extra-special 'golden handshake' leaked to the newspapers. Of course, in the gossip of the workplace, a debate began among those of us who still had a few years to do before we retired concerning whether we would get what was owed to us as well.

If there had been a court battle, if the issue had been aired in public, then a precedent would have been seen to be set, and it would have been impossible for others on the Rushdie teams not to have had a similar entitlement. The way it was handled was not good news for us but we hoped the Met would do the decent thing by us. They didn't. It was gossiped that our overtime documents had been lost so as far as I was concerned there would be no backup for any claim. So I just got on with the job. And that turned out to be even more galling.

I went with Scruffy to a regular update meeting with MI6 at Millbank. He was briefed on the current mood in Iran and the wider Islamic world towards him, and on possible threats from home-grown terrorists. He was told the threat was still high; intelligence reported it was mainly from a lone assassin, a Jackal type who wanted to make a name for himself as well as avenging Allah. The good news was that the Iranian government were not actively seeking to carry out the fatwa. The Iranians, after so many years in the wilderness, wanted more dialogue with the West.

With Khomeini dead and a more pro-Western leader in place, the atmosphere was more settled. I stood at the back of the room listening intently to this, briefly thinking about how far we had come from those early days, when I heard something that brought me back into reality. Scruffy said he wanted to publish a book about his life under this death sentence and his experiences of being protected by Special Branch.

The diary!

He'd done it, written a book about us all – and might make a bucketful of money.

His MI6 case officer was bemused but calm and to the point. I was in the room as Scruffy was told it would not be a good idea for him to publish his book at this time. It would only inflame feelings against him and give the impression that he was, again, making a profit out of his alleged blasphemy.

That was that. For then. Nearly twenty years on from the fatwa, he's even more of a celebrity. He married Elizabeth West and they had a son, Milan. When he married for the fourth time, to the exotic Padma Lakshmi – she left him in 2007 after three years – he had a 'hen' party with his friends Kylie and Dannii Minogue, Mariella Frostrup, the author Kathy Lette and cookery queen Nigella Lawson, with whom he was once infamously photographed jiving.

Scruffy on the dance floor. It made me smile. As did his interview in April 2008 with the UK edition of *Esquire* magazine. When it was suggested to him that a book detailing his protection days might be dull, he replied, 'Oh, you'd be surprised how much incident there was, how little of it came into the public domain. There's a huge untold story.'

I've given you an exclusive preview, as much as is secure, of Salman Rushdie's untold story, of a book I'm sure he'll someday offer. It is ever pertinent to our lives today. After 9/11, we are all, as he has said, living under a fatwa.

In that Esquire interview he offered these thoughts: 'You know in the Hitchcock movie *The Birds*? The first crow that flutters across the sky? Well, that was me and now the roof has fallen through. I was a harbinger of things to come.

'It's just sad that so many people had to die in order for people to understand what happened to me wasn't a random event.

'I tried to argue a lot in those days that this event was among one of many. I wasn't the only writer being attacked by radical Islam. Others were killed. But that was seen as special pleading, as me trying to excuse myself. There was a very large assumption that I was the architect of my own misfortune,' he said.

Nevertheless, in June 2007, Salman Rushdie was knighted in the Queen's Birthday Honours. My first thought was, Arise, Sir Scruffy! My second thought was, What a security nightmare it would be if he ever ventured to Buckingham Palace to collect his honour! In fact he collected it from Her Majesty in late June 2008, apparently without incident.

I had to wonder at the wisdom when after all the millions he had cost the British taxpayer it looked like another raspberry to the Muslim world. Indeed, they reacted quickly with the Iranian government denouncing the knighthood as 'an obvious example of fighting against Islam by high-ranking British officials'.

In another flashback to the fatwa, the Pakistani Parliament passed a resolution condemning the knighthood, the Minister of Religious Affairs decreeing that it would justify future suicide bombings. In the *Guardian* – where else? – a dozen British Muslim groups called it a 'deliberate provocation and insult to 1.5 billion Muslims around the world'.

Sir Salman said, 'I am thrilled and humbled to receive this great honour, and am very grateful that my work has been recognised in this way.'

Yet a month after his gong was announced he wasn't having much of a time of it, having been dumped by his fourth wife and getting a critical drubbing for his novel *The Enchantress of Florence*. Peter Kemp, in his *Sunday Times* review in April 2008, was less than enchanted: 'Rushdie seeks to keep the reader aware that his guiding inspiration is "The Thousand and One Nights",' he wrote. Sadly, by the time you reach the end of this novel with its garish banalities and depthless sensationalism, what you're most aware of are the 1,001 ways in which is would have been more profitable and enjoyable to pass the time.'

Shortly after that review appeared he gave an interview to *The Spectator* in London and talked about *Midnight's Children* in comparison with his latest work. 'I did feel there was an awful lot riding on that book,' he said, 'and fortunately people thought it was OK. I felt the same thing with this. When I finished it I thought, By any standard that I know, this is a good book, and if people don't agree with me, I will be really devastated. Because it would show that there is either something wrong with the world, or something wrong with me.'

Chapter Seven
Home Affairs

'I value them all tremendously, and not just
for the security.'

Norman Tebbit on his Special Branch protection team
three years after the attempted assassination of Margaret
Thatcher and her Cabinet in Brighton in 1984

There is something wrong in a world where you have to
police a tightrope which is so often stretched to the limit
by evil.

In the political world there are many brave men and
women who are pilloried in public but behind-the-scenes
make big decisions which affect us all and often put them
under threat.

Yes, there are some real tossers too.

When I left the topsy-turvy world of Salman Rushdie I was
attached to the Home Office and served three secretaries of
state, Ken Baker, Ken Clarke and Michael Howard. All three
were totally different characters. Baker was a well-read man,
often giving an apt quote from some literary giant from
centuries past. Ken Clarke had the image of the beer-
swilling, cigar-smoking, sport-loving chap. And, yes,
Michael Howard did have 'something of the night about

him', but the ardent football fan did have to get his teeth into some brutal political situations.

Politically, it was a busy department, which meant I was busy too. Every visit had to be preplanned and advance work completed. The most dangerous were prison visits, not only for a home secretary but for his SB guys as well. What's a Category 1 prisoner thinking when he's presented with the double whammy of a Tory home secretary who is traditionally hard on crime and a copper? All that was needed was a well-aimed bowl of urine or a spit in the face and he would have been very pleased with his morning's work and given extra rations of drugs, cigarettes and food.

I was with Ken Baker when he was being shown around a prison workshop. I and another officer, Keith, had deposited our guns at the prison gates in case we were attacked and our weapons used against us. Ken Baker was talking to an inmate who was making Tiffany lamps and was holding a rather fetching purple shard of glass. I was standing right next to the Home Secretary waiting for this lifer to make a nasty mess of either one of us.

The bizarrely tattooed prisoner wasn't the most talkative of people – hardly surprising, really – but he had a determined look in his eye. I was ready to push Baker out of the way if he did attack. Ken Baker could have been at the Chelsea Flower Show.

He was a cool guy. When a massive bomb ripped through the heart of the City of London he immediately decided to visit the scene.

Special Branch were acutely aware of the threat to mainland Britain in the early months of 1993. We'd received intelligence that the Provisional IRA had sufficient personnel, equipment and the means to carry out and maintain a sustained bombing campaign. The PIRA had close links to the Spanish terrorist group ETA.

They allegedly received some funds from Libyan sources. Libya's good ol' Colonel Muammar al-Gaddafi was then guarded by female, blue-uniformed, close-protection officers armed with AK-47s, nail varnish, perfume and lipstick. Also helping the terror campaign were funds from equally misguided Irish Americans. Even with this threat – and everyone knowing about it – we in Special Branch and the other security services were still poorly armed and poorly trained.

In March 1993 a white Ford van was stolen in Newcastle-under-Lyme and sprayed blue. One ton of fertiliser bomb made by the South Armagh Brigade had been smuggled into England and was hidden on the van under a layer of tarmac. On 24 April the van was driven by two volunteers and parked outside the Hong Kong and Shanghai Bank in the City. These ASU killers were driven away by car by a third volunteer. A number of bomb warnings were given with a recognised code word and the area was evacuated. There were six recognised code words that defined certain places and incidents in the PIRA 'struggle'. SB and the Anti-Terrorist Branch, and now MI5, know from which word is given whether it is going to be a large or small blast.

At 10.25 a.m. the bomb went off, injuring forty-four people and killing a freelance photographer, Ed Henty, who was working for the *News of the World*. The explosion shook buildings and shattered hundreds of windows, sending glass showering down into the streets below. It was similar to the bomb that devastated the Baltic Exchange, killing three people, a year earlier. Repairs to the Exchange had just been completed, and the building reopened, when the same institutions were damaged again.

A medieval church, St Ethelburga's, collapsed; another church and Liverpool Street Underground station were also wrecked. The blast did more than £1 billion in damage.

At the time there were bomb scares almost nightly in the City but it was after the Bishopsgate bomb that the PIRA peace process was started in 1993. On the Sunday evening I got a call to go back into work.

The Home Secretary wanted to visit the bomb site. He didn't want any publicity or any special arrangements made for his visit. We informed the control rooms at Scotland Yard and under the cover of darkness made our way to the outer security cordons set up at the site. We had to use a particular route, not only to ensure our safety but also to ensure that we didn't destroy vital evidence. We were stopped at these cordons but were quickly let through. As we neared the seat of the explosion we stopped and made contact with the senior police, fire and forensics officers.

Ken Baker was genuinely moved and surprised by the devastation. I know I was. There was an eerie silence and teams were talking in hushed voices. The street lights gave it another sinister dimension. It was a sea of glass.

I was walking behind the main group on half a dozen inches deep of broken glass and debris. Whole office blocks and the surrounding buildings had lost their windows and in some the blinds were blowing about in the breeze.

We got close to where the seat of the bomb was, but Ken Baker stopped. He didn't want the forensic teams distracted from their work. They were looking for parts of the van and the bomb. Anything that was found was identified and bagged ready to be sent to Fort Halstead in Kent for further scrutiny. (Remnants of the Pan Am jumbo blown up over Lockerbie in December 1988 were still at Fort Halstead.)

From the tiniest fragments, the perpetrator can be identified, because each bomb maker has his or her own way, a 'fingerprint', of putting a lethal device together. It was very unnerving because we had no idea whether, as with an earthquake, there might be an 'aftershock' from another planted bomb.

The Home Secretary was not a man to be intimidated. He was a canny political player. I closely witnessed him in action during the 1992 general election campaign. Elections are very tiring, as we had to go from one end of the country to the other with barely a few hours' sleep, but adrenalin kept us all going. The Conservative Party under John Major was fighting to stay in power against a determined bid by the Kinnock-led Labour Party. The Conservatives had held onto government since Thatcher became Britain's first female Prime Minister on 4 May 1979 (she resigned in November 1990).

The inside story from Central Office to the Home Secretary was that they thought that it would be a good idea to lose the election; many thought they would, and John Major's victory came as a great surprise to them. And him.

We went to Cheltenham to raise the profile of the Tory candidate John Taylor, now Lord Taylor. We visited local schools to meet parents and press the flesh and drove around waving to the electorate as well as meeting the local press.

The big political threat to the Tories was from the Liberals, who were spending huge amounts of money and targeting the Tory marginals. In our car Ken Baker and John Taylor were bemoaning the scurrilous campaign being run by the Liberals. Taylor, who is black, was a respected lawyer and had worked for the Tories for many years behind the scenes. Some of the Liberal campaign literature had racist overtones and Baker was incensed by that. He threatened to take the Liberals to court over the campaign. Taylor rejected that idea. He wanted to fight the campaign head on and deal with it in his own way.

By happy chance, Kelvin MacKenzie, the editor of the *Sun*, had a story ready to print about the Liberals. And, as if sensing Ken Baker's disquiet by osmosis, he did.

The *Sun*'s front page of 6 February 1992 had a shriek of a headline: It's Paddy Pantsdown. The slightly smaller front-page headlines had this from the Liberal leader Paddy Ashdown: I had a 5-month fling with my secretary. And from his wife: We've been happy for thirty years. Not, clearly, that happy. To emphasise his coup about the Liberal leader's sexual affair with his secretary, MacKenzie had gone to town inside the paper: the front-page strap announced, 'The Ashdown Affair: Pages 2, 3, 4, 5, 6, 7, 8, 9.' It was classic personality politics. The Tory-supporting Rupert Murdoch *Sun* would strike again on polling day with the front page shouting on 9 April 1992, If Kinnock wins today will the last person to leave Britain please turn out the lights. Neil Kinnock's head stared out at the readers from a light bulb.

Kinnock was dead in the water. Sadly, and surprisingly, a little later so was Ken Baker. A Cabinet reshuffle was announced and out he went, to be replaced by another Ken, Ken Clarke. His constituency was West Bridgeford on the outskirts of Nottingham, different from the genteel streets of Dorking and the Mole Valley where I'd been with Ken Baker. He was a man of the people, liked a beer with a cigar, jazz, birdwatching, football (Nottingham Forest), cricket, boxing and motor racing. He was not the most smartly dressed of ministers. When he had to attend formal occasions and wear a morning suit with tails, he topped off his ensemble by wearing his trade mark Hush Puppies with the laces undone.

He liked talking – and Blackpool. We were in the car with one of his female advisers when he cheered on about a visit to this seaside resort. He'd been given a batch of Blackpool rock with his name stamped through it. He said he would raffle it for children in his constituency. His aide liked that idea and told him, 'And all the youngsters can say they sucked on Ken Clarke!'

The Home Secretary simply stared at her and then looked straight at me. An eyebrow was raised and the subject of Blackpool rock was deemed taboo.

One of his first major problems was too many spies. His own. The Cold War was finished and MI5 had dozens of underemployed spooks on the books. The head of MI5 had direct access to the Prime Minister and took advantage by putting a case forward for the spies from Toad Hall, MI5, to take the lead role of fighting the IRA away from us. The government agreed and SB lost their role, but not all the files.

He also got heavily involved in international spookery when Special Branch uncovered a plot to blow up John Major on a trip to Delhi. Sikh terrorists planned to plant four bombs at India's Republic Day celebrations, at which Major was to be guest of honour, the first British leader to attend the parade since Indian independence in 1947. It was decided the visit would go ahead. Ken Clarke had prepared the way for this piece of diplomacy on a visit to India a few weeks earlier, when an extradition treaty had been agreed.

This was security again and, behind the scenes, the Branch worked with the Indian security services, who had a marvellous internal intelligence network. They discovered a cache of sophisticated arms and bombs. What got everyone excited was a trigger device for the explosives. It had been put together in Japan and smuggled into India through Canada. The bombs – a huge one was to be planted under the main platform, where Major would sit for four hours with Indian Prime Minister Narasimha Rao – were to be operated by this remote-control device.

It was quite a co-operation coup for the Home Secretary and Special Branch for only a couple hours after the Prime Minister's arrival in Delhi one of the ringleaders was arrested. He led the authorities to a 'safe' house where three members of the Sikh militant Khalistan Commando Force, from the northern Punjab state, were hiding. Despite the plot being broken up the SB protection officers were on red alert, all the time crucially mindful of Major's safety.

Michael Howard was a hardline Home Secretary. He was one of the few ministers who tried to persuade Margaret Thatcher to fight on in November 1990. He was also adamant that Tony Blair should not have released the IRA prisoners as part of the Good Friday Agreement. His viewpoint was that, if the government released these prisoners, then they would not have a bargaining tool.

When he was Home Secretary he used to sign the authority for the phone taps and surveillance on suspected terrorists. He was also against repatriating IRA prisoners held on the UK mainland back to Northern Ireland. These actions made him more of a target and he received protection long after he left office.

It was Anne Widdecombe who had said Howard had 'something of the night about him', and politically that was the case, but he was a pleasure to be with, always very considerate, along with his children and his wife, the former model Sandra Paul. When my first son was born he sent flowers to my wife, congratulating her on the birth.

When he was appointed Home Secretary, he didn't want SB protection. When we on the team heard this we had nightmares – not about his safety, for it was far more important than that: we would be put out of a job and would be heading back to the Yard to sit around filling in on other teams. Working at the Home Office was a very good posting, always busy and always interesting.

As the new Home Secretary, he went into Queen Anne Gate and upstairs to meet his new private office staff, along with one of our senior officers from A Squad and someone from Toad Hall, to discuss security. It was explained to him what he had to do regarding security and he realised that it would be best to have a protection team with him. He had one stipulation: he couldn't sit in the back of the car, since he worked in the car and sitting in the back would make him sick.

It was agreed that he could sit in the front and he did from then on. It caused problems from time to time. As we arrived at some venues the photographers would start to take pictures of me getting out of the car while the Home Secretary got out of the front seat and just laughed.

At the Home Office he inherited a spectacular mess from Ken Clarke who – infuriated by what he considered to be incompetent leadership and inflexible working practices – had set up an inquiry into police conditions under Sir Patrick Sheehy. Later, Clarke would get a directorship on the board of Sheehy's British American Tobacco company, but first his successor had to deal with the dreadful relations between the police and the government. Howard didn't agree with the Sheehy inquiry but couldn't ditch a policy from his predecessor and had to go along with it. Every day in the papers there was talk of police unrest and the outcry over the proposals. A mass protest was staged at Wembley.

In the car on the morning of the protest, Howard asked me what I felt about it. I told him that I was going to go. He was surprised and asked if he should go. I said not to, because he would only come out of it looking bad from a policy that had been thrust upon him. I said I would give him a full match report.

Along with a few thousand other police officers, I attended the protest with senior officers giving their opinions. The politicians were there, including the Labour Party spokesperson – step forward Anthony Charles Lynton Blair.

He blew it. A perfect time to send out a message of support for the police and all we got was Labour Party crap. We sat there in silence. At least the ladies of the Women's Institute booed him. The WI were far more outspoken than police officers; God help us if the WI ever start a riot!

In the speech we had a glimpse of what Blair would be like if he got the top job. It was all about him and presentation. Forget the issues and the problem – let's talk about how good I am. I formed my view about Mr Tony Blair right there and then and it hasn't changed. Tosser.

As soon as Michael Howard got in the car the following morning, I told him it was a good meeting, which was not how the Home Office had envisaged it. They wanted it to be full of hotheads sounding off, an ill-disciplined affair, a waste of time, proving that the police needed to be brought into line.

I said that the strength of feeling against the changes shown by the highly motivated campaign by the Police Federation (the coppers' trade union for ranks up to and including chief inspector) were very strong. He listened carefully. Sir Patrick's key proposal was performance- (or appraisal-) related pay and it was roundly defeated. Few, if any, of the other recommendations were implemented.

One Sunday afternoon, Howard was at his constituency home in Kent. He and his wife had to attend a function in the afternoon but when I arrived to take them to the event she was missing. She'd been stung on the tongue by a wasp and was in great pain. I offered a remedy: drink milk as alkaline, which would ease the sting.

A few days later I met his wife Sandra, who has quite a pronounced stammer, and asked about her sting. She told me that they were in the garden with friends having lunch and she was eating vanilla and blueberry ice cream. She thought that the wasp was a blueberry and ate it; needless to say the wasp wasn't up for the idea of being eaten and stung her on the tongue. I asked her if she had any after-effects and she said that it was OK, it just made her talk funny.

There were not that many moments to bring a gentle smile. Especially when intelligence told us the IRA were planning an outrage during a Conservative Party conference – in Brighton. Nearly a decade on from what might have been the PIRA's finest hour – the assassination of Maggie and her Cabinet at Brighton's Grand Hotel – this sinister scenario was being played out again. This time it was meant to be John Major and his government, who were at that very hotel. The

Sussex police had established a security cordon around the conference hotel and hall, and no one and nothing moved in or out without some kind of pass or accreditation.

My Special Branch team were 'parachuted' in to work with the Sussex coppers, who would guide us around the town if we had to leave the secure area for a meeting or dinner. It was normal procedure on out-of-towners to have this kind of help. It was not only for the nightmare scenario but in case of accidents or roadworks. The locals, in theory, could steer us around anything that might delay us. Then these guys would know how to get around the problem.

We met them in a lay-by outside town and we followed the unmarked car straight to the Grand Hotel. Most of the time there was no need for cars, as all the conference and fringe meetings would take place within the ring of steel set up by the police. During the final session there was to be the traditional keynote speech from the leader – Major in this case. The whole of the Cabinet were on the platform and the protection teams were standing to one side. As the PM was giving his speech I noticed that all the teams were starting to steal glances at each other and pass on signals. An A Squad senior had been told by SB control room that the IRA were planning to mount an attack. The information acknowledged they couldn't do anything in Brighton, but were going to blow up and kill a senior government minister after the conference.

The whole Cabinet were here in Brighton. Who was the senior minister they were going to try to kill? We had no idea or way of knowing; all we could do was make plans on how to get out of town. The protection teams would leave at different times and go by different routes. No protected person would be in the same road as another. This put enormous pressure on our Sussex colleagues. I followed the lead car all over Brighton to do some 'dry cleaning'.

The tension was mounting and the local hospital was put on standby to expect casualties. Just in case.

All the protection teams took their principals out of Brighton at speed. We had to keep our vigilance up, since it could have been a decoy to mount an attack elsewhere. As the teams went into each police force area, we called the local control room to alert them to our whereabouts. Someone said we were lucky, but that remark harshly reminded me of the statement from the IRA after the 1984 Brighton bomb: 'We were unlucky tonight but you have to be lucky all the time.'

It was an accurate assessment. But it also highlighted for me some of the astonishingly resilient people the IRA were attacking and we were protecting. Norman Tebbit's wife, Margaret, was crippled in the Brighton bomb and he was severely injured. Later, when he talked about it and his protection team he offered, 'I don't think I'm meant to say how many bodyguards I have, but there is a team and I have got to know them very well over the years. They are all marvellous characters and there is a fund of family jokes that includes them. I have just lost the chap who was with me at the time of the Brighton bombing. I value them all tremendously and not just for the security.

'When Margaret was in hospital I was living a rather lonely life and at times not a very easy life. I was often very glad of their friendship and company as well as the security.'

Norman, now Lord, Tebbit told of when he and his wife were having physiotherapy at the marvellous Stoke Mandeville Hospital in Aylesbury. It was pretty gruelling treatment and their limbs were being pulled and stretched. One of our team looking after them looked into the treatment room and in a threatening voice shouted, 'If you sign the confession we'll call them off!'

Chapter Eight
Badlands

'Governments, politicians and generals are
leading the world with their eyes wide shut.'
Stanley Kubrick, film director, 1996

It wasn't unusual for Home Office staff to go out for a lunchtime drink at the Buck or the Feathers, but generally they didn't down a bottle of wine and take an unmarked Special Branch car from the 'secure' underground car park at Scotland Yard.

Michael Howard's personal aide, Janine Barnes, did that with ease. She got in the Mondeo, which had the keys in the ignition – common practice at the Yard to allow cars to be moved in emergencies – and reversed out of the bay. She then bounced off a Vauxhall Cavalier, which collided with another Cavalier.

She smashed into both cars – one belonged to Commander David Tucker, head of the Anti-Terrorist Branch, the other to Commander George Churchill-Coleman, head of the Fraud Squad – a second time before hitting the accelerator and taking off out of the car park. She abandoned the Ford a few miles away, then hitched a lift in a lorry to Brixton police station, where she reported her handbag lost. She said nothing about losing the plot.

Janine, who organised Michael Howard's diary, was convicted of aggravated vehicle taking and driving without insurance, and later banned from driving for 18 months and made to do a hundred hours' community service. Her drunken car-crash spree was a huge embarrassment to the Home Secretary. I'd recently been head-hunted away from the Home Office and was looking after the former Secretary of State for Northern Ireland, Tom King, who'd served at a most controversial time. He was not an easy man.

The biggest workload for A Squad during the 1990s resulted from the terrorist threat from the Provisional IRA. Tom King was the number-one target on their assassination top ten. He'd been the Secretary of State for Defence under John Major during the 1991 Gulf War but was now a backbencher. Yet he retained round-the-clock security. His qualifications for the dubious honour of being on the IRA Most Wanted list were many, but specifically he was in Maggie's government, which, following the death of hunger striker Bobby Sands in 1981, was still reason enough. He was also in office as Northern Ireland Secretary when the East Tyrone Brigade of the PIRA were ambushed and killed by the SAS in 1987.

The IRA were happy to murder people but a shoot-to-kill policy by the other side made them furious and vengeful. Yet shoot-to-kill was nothing new. In 1980 I'd not been a copper for too long when, on 30 April, half a dozen terrorists took over the Iranian Embassy in London. It made the world sit up and take notice of the SAS and their Operation Nimrod; they even made a movie, *Who Dares Wins* (which is the SAS's motto), about the six-day siege, which ended when the SAS stormed the building.

I was acutely aware of it because of the plight of a fellow PC, Constable Trevor Lock, who was on official protection duty at the embassy's main entrance in Prince's Gate, South Kensington in central London, and became one of the original twenty-six hostages. It could have been any of us.

The terrorist team calling itself the 'Democratic Revolutionary Movement for the Liberation of Arabistan' – oh, they love their titles! – demanded the release of ninety-one of their comrades held in Iranian jails. It turned truly horrid. Hostage negotiators bartered with supplies of food and cigarettes, and on the third day the BBC broadcast a statement by the terrorists following threats to kill a hostage. On Day Six the terrorists did kill a hostage, press attaché Abbas Lavasani, and threw his body outside.

Maggie Thatcher went ballistic. The order to deploy a unit of the Counter Revolutionary Warfare (CRW) wing of the SAS was issued at the start of the siege. When Abbas Lavasani was shot, the Metropolitan Police Commissioner, David McNee, told the Ministry of Defence this outrage was now a 'military operation'.

It has been reported that before the SAS went in, the landing paths of planes into Heathrow were lowered and British Gas drilled in a nearby street to provide noise cover, the terrorists and hostages were spied on through fibre-optic probes inserted into a shared wall and sensitive microphones were used to listen in from that building. The raid had been rehearsed in a mock-up 'Iranian Embassy' at a nearby army barracks. The real thing began on Bank Holiday Monday, 5

May, just twenty-three minutes after Abbas Lavasani's body had been dismissively thrown out of the Embassy.

You could never accuse Maggie of being indecisive. Or the SAS. There was an explosion in the stairwell, electric power was cut in that second and the SAS boys and stun grenades came flying through the upper floors with explosive charges blowing out window frames.

With Heckler & Koch MP5 submachine guns at fire-ready, the SAS troops took over. Five of the six terrorists were killed; one was later found to have been shot twenty-seven times. The SAS worked to their own agenda.

But back to Tom King. Information was received that the PIRA were going to drive a JCB earth mover into a police station in Loughgall, County Armagh, and take out everyone inside. Tom King ordered the SAS to intercept and ambush the attackers. An earlier IRA attack had used a JCB digger, its front bucket packed with explosives, to ram into a police station before exploding. Reports of a stolen JCB, combined with other intelligence, convinced us that a similar attack was planned.

The special intelligence unit of the Royal Ulster Constabulary (RUC), E4A, located the stolen digger and suspected that the IRA East Tyrone ASU were involved. Intelligence also told of a blue Toyota van being stolen by masked men, probably to be used to carry IRA gunmen to provide covering fire during the attack. The JCB was seen being driven from its hiding place in a local farm.

Over two days the coppers stationed at Loughgall were 'exchanged' for the SAS, who wore RUC uniforms and reported for duty at the normal times. An SAS ambush force was concealed behind a row of trees that ran alongside the road past the station; several cut-off groups were placed to cover possible escape routes.

They were mostly armed with Heckler & Koch G3 assault rifles. The 7.62mm round fired by the G3 had greater stopping power than either the M16 rifles or MP5 submachine guns usually carried by the SAS.

At 7 p.m., the Toyota van was spotted on a scouting drive around the station. It drove on but returned in three minutes followed by the JCB, which had three men in its cab and a huge oil drum in its front bucket. The secret SAS squad watched the JCB crash through the wire fence around the station and the three men, all hooded, jumped from the cab and one of them lit a fuse on the oil drum. As they ran off from the JCB, the doors of the Toyota swung open and five armed men leaped out and started spraying the police station with bullets.

The SAS went into action, starting a ferocious firefight. The troopers riddled the gunmen, the bombers and the van with bullets. It lasted only a few seconds, but that hail of gunfire killed all eight IRA men. The explosives packed into the JCB's bucket exploded, wrecking the police station. It was a killing field. Around 250 bullets went into the van alone. During a later SB operation, the general officer in command in the Province, General Sir John Wilsey, told me, 'Even the army is facing cutbacks. If not, there would have been a lot more bullets.'

As a military operation it was a great coup. Politically, as always, there were shades of opinion. It was a tough line, which would deter support for the IRA. Or it would make more people join the terrorists. It did shake up the IRA commanders concerned about our sharp intelligence, troubled by the security breach that had led to the ambush.

It was not luck. A shoot-to-kill policy was in place, as the Iranian Embassy siege had demonstrated.

Tom King would be a big notch on an IRA gun. As Northern Ireland Secretary he was truly persona non grata with the terrorist outfit. Operation Octavian was in force at the Yard and all military property, including career-information shops and people mentioned on death lists, like Tom King, would have their property checked twenty-four hours a day. This task was immense and was shared with local police authorities.

A PIRA active service unit were arrested in 1987 on King's Wiltshire farm; they were later convicted of conspiracy to murder him. Despite this, Tom King – now Lord King of Bridgwater and for seven years until 2001 the chairman of the Intelligence and Security Committee – would seldom tell us anything about his movements. We could not make the most basic of security arrangements. He said to me, 'If no one knows what I'm doing, then the IRA won't know either.'

OK, but this surely didn't extend to the guys who were trying to keep him alive! He hardly ever told us a thing. This made life difficult for the protection teams, for he treated us in the most incredible way. Even down on the farm he loved.

As soon as he agreed to protection – if they don't want it then they don't get it, simple as that – we found ourselves spending many hours in the country. There was plenty of good, clean air and there was plenty to keep us occupied on the farm – an amazing contrast to our roles as A Squad trained-to-kill specialist officers. I got plenty of exercise cutting back bushes and tree branches and feeding them into a shredder. We built pheasant pens, were beaters on shoots, herded sheep, moved pig pens from field to field and so on. It was like childhood, playing farmers. I suppose you could say we were undercover.

All the Special Branch armed officers were given £350 allowances to buy country gear. We had to be in the open and we required this extra clothing to be comfortable on the farm. I went to the gentlemen's sports shop, Farlow's in Pall Mall, and bought a Barbour waxed jacket with lining, waterproof leggings and Timberland boots.

Tom King supplied wellingtons for his armed guards down on the farm in beautiful countryside near Bath in Wiltshire. Not much was grown, as the land has been designated as set-aside land under EU farming regulations and he was subsidised by the EU for not farming. Other farmers used the land for their cows to graze.

He farmed pigs, to be slaughtered for his family's consumption. The pigs were given names. One was TINA as in the Margaret Thatcher era of There Is No Alternative. Another was Soames, after Nicholas Soames, the rotund former Defence Minister and Prince Charles's friend. King would gambol around the farm shouting 'Soames, Soames!' and hugely enjoy himself. Whatever turns you on, I suppose.

The police security post was one of the cottages on the farm; one of the bedrooms was used as a changing room for the team to change into farming gear.

We spent time building pheasant pens, some of them quite big, at various locations all over the land. We cleared the trees and bushes and took down the previous year's pens before building new ones. It was an economical business. Where possible, materials were recycled and used more than once. The staples used to hold the netting to the wooden supports were not hammered all the way in. By doing it this way they could be pulled out by pliers and used again. If the staple was bent, it could be straightened. Farmer Tom helped me out sometimes when I didn't quite grasp the method.

Once the pens were ready the last job was to put electrical wire around the perimeter to stop foxes getting in. Two wires were placed above one another about six inches apart, connected to a transformer fixed to a twelve-volt car battery.

With the pens ready, the chicks were delivered and we would go back at 7 p.m. to make sure all was well. We always kept quiet, silent if possible, so as not to upset the chicks. One of the biggest pens was on one side of Hidden Valley in the trees. The ground was loose with shale and chalk and we were always losing our footings.

When we arrived at the pen the light on the battery terminal was flashing. King was concerned. I picked up a blade of grass and touched the wire. By doing this I would still have got a shock but not as big as if I had held the wire with my bare hands. The wire was dead, no current and no shock.

'Bugger!' said King adding, 'We need water.'

And he turned and went to get a bucket of water, which he threw over the earth terminal, which was rammed into the ground attached to a spanner. I tested it again. Nothing.

'But the light's flashing!' wailed King.

'Yes, there's a current from the battery to the transformer but a current isn't getting from the transformer to the fence.'

'Yes, you're quite right. Jim, you come with me and we'll check to see if there isn't a short circuit on the fence.'

Off they went and I took hold of the transformer, opened it up and fiddled with it and put it back together again. I picked up a blade of grass and – shit! Shaking my hand with the shock, I realised it was working.

At that moment, from the peace and tranquillity of the still summer evening, was a full throated cry of pain.

I called out, 'It's working!'

By then, King, who was wearing shorts, had lost his footing and slid into the now live electric fence and the sight was something out of a Tom and Jerry cartoon with Farmer Tom slipping and sliding as he tried to get his legs off the fence.

During that period we carried out a mixed bunch of chores, including sheep dipping. One day was spent pulling ragwort, a notifiable weed, from one of his fields. It was good to get the ragwort out for if a jobsworth from the Ministry of Agriculture saw it he or she might get the farm closed down.

Apple-picking was also on the list of jobs at the end of this exceptional tour of duty. I felt like an extra in the Darling Buds of May. We were in the orchard doing this when we had a cloudburst of tropical proportions. We all clambered for cover; the only one not to find any shelter was the former minister. He stood there like a drowned rat. He looked at me and said in a disgruntled voice, 'I'm soaking wet.'

'So I can see sir, but I've got to keep my powder dry.'

From dredging the river on his farm to stacking bales of hay for winter feed, it was all part of life down on the farm.

King certainly provided entertainment, as did his wife Jane, Baroness King of Bridgwater. We had installed a system of infrared cameras throughout the property and one of our guys nailed a sensor to a tree. She said to him: 'Don't you know that's how you give trees AIDS?'

It was news to him.

During the Parliamentary summer recess King would play golf with the House of Commons and Lords Golf Society. He was due to play at Ganton Golf Club in Scarborough but was late as usual. He invited me to play with him, since his friends had already started. I put my gun in my golf bag and went out to play. The rest of the protection team went off to check into our hotel. We had some laughs, since, for each of the first nine holes, he visited every bunker.

At the nineteenth hole, knowing he was staying at someone's house close by, I asked what he was doing for the evening, thinking he would stay there for the evening after a long drive and a round of golf. Wrong. He said his host had arranged a small gathering. We took him to his overnight accommodation and he told us to wait. I was still in shorts and a golf shirt.

About an hour later he came out in a suit. I opened the car door and he got in. He told me to go the village hall and he directed his long-suffering driver, Don, from the Government Car Service, to the location.

There are laid-down procedures that I had to follow when out of the Metropolitan Police District. Special Branch has national responsibility, but with it are certain protocols. The first is that when we are in another force area, in this case West Yorkshire, I must tell that force that we are on their turf and that I am armed, in case of an incident; I don't want to get shot by the local force.

Tom King hated having too many uniformed police around and would fly into rages over this. His protection teams tried to maintain normal working procedures but with our weak management it wasn't a fair contest.

On this occasion I'd told the local sheriff that we were on their ground and that we didn't want any help. Normal practice would be that, during the night, the local police would stay in the house where he was staying to provide security while we get some rest. But with King this was not easy.

As we got closer to the venue I could see a lot of cars for a small gathering. I looked in my rear-view mirror and he was looking the other way. I was getting angry and over the radio I quietly said to the backup team, 'Another piss-take.'

We pulled into the car park of the village hall in rural Yorkshire. The place was packed. It was a Tory Party fundraiser on the rubber-chicken circuit. I got out of the car fuming and opened his door, let him out, then slammed the car door behind him. I followed him into the hall and there they all were.

A Tory worthy was collecting tickets at the door from the two hundred people invited to the event and King was guest of honour. He didn't look at me and walked straight into the venue. I followed him in. My gun was now in a gun bag, which I draped over my shoulder for all to see.

I stood in the doorway resplendent in my golfing attire and totally underdressed for the occasion but I stayed there and watched him go to the top table and take his seat. He never looked in my direction. I turned and said to the team, 'Fuck him, let's go and get something to eat.'

We were experienced with the King mindset; you had to roll with the punches, otherwise you'd go mad. I put in a call to the Yard saying that protection had been removed, just in case anything happened. I was determined to have my say over the issue. I was prepared to stand up to him and argue my corner.

After the event, he got back into the car and I turned to him and said, 'About tonight, sir. You let me down over this. I've worked with you for a number of years and I know your feelings over having armed policeman running all over the place, but you didn't allow me to do the minimum requirements of my job.

'You knew what was going on and you didn't even have the courtesy of telling me. There could have been anybody at this event, even the chief constable of the local force, and, when he asks me why his officers or control room were not informed, what do I tell him? Tonight you could have got me sacked from the job, all because you think that you know best. Well you don't. I'm not impressed.'

I turned around in my seat and faced the front.

He said, 'Er, yes, you're right, I'm sorry about that. It won't happen again.'

I didn't reply. I called the Yard and told them that protection was now back in place, so that he could hear me. It took patience as well as mental gymnastics to keep one jump ahead of him.

Every now and then we did get our own back. His daughter was due to be married, and, the evening before the big day, Father held a drinks party for friends coming from all over the country to enjoy the weekend's celebrations. He'd asked a farm-hand to make signs giving directions to his farm. He asked the SB team to post them all around the area. Strangely, some of the signs pointed in the wrong direction and cars were heading all over the county of Wiltshire.

The antithesis of King was Roy Mason, now Lord Mason of Barnsley. He was the model principal. When he said that he would be out at 5 p.m. he was out. He also kept us informed of his movements and his plans. Weekends with the good lord who remained a target out of office were good, too. He would regularly have a small beer with Seth from *Emmerdale* or former cricket umpire Dickie Bird. What I did notice about his small group of Yorkshire friends was that they all bought their own drinks, apart from Dickie, who would buy a round for everybody and Mason would reciprocate.

Roy Mason had been the Northern Ireland Secretary in Harold Wilson's government and he had brought the SAS into the Province. His plan was to crush the PIRA in South Armagh and it was working. There were fewer killings and Mason's tactics didn't go down well with the PIRA.

What do they say about not changing something that works? The plan hit the buffers when the Home Secretary, Merlyn Rees, argued in a Cabinet meeting that the SAS should be deployed throughout the entire Province. His argument won, and, instead of concentrating their efforts in Armagh, the SAS had to spread themselves much more thinly over the whole of the six counties. Mason kept his Special Branch protection for more than thirty years. When there was a threat to remove his protection team, they would let him know and he would put an article in one of the daily newspapers, generally saying that the only good terrorist is a dead one. Hey presto! His profile would rise and the protection would remain in place. Everyone was happy, including the protection team, who loved their weekends in Barnsley.

It wasn't so pleasant, and it certainly wasn't cricket, more like warfare, protecting Northern Ireland Secretaries when they were in office and dealing daily with the IRA. Often, what went on symbolised for me the erosion of personal and political freedom in the ever-ongoing struggle for security.

In 2002, I joined a Special Branch team and we travelled between London and Belfast with occasional American assignments. The Northern Ireland Office was alongside MI5 on Millbank on the north side of the Thames.

We were clearly VIPs – our office, with just about enough room to swing a cat, was in the basement of the building. We had telephones and basic Internet, which was monitored by the spooks next door, four beat-up lockers and a gun safe. It was like something from the past, a chapter from *The Ipcress File*, not a Bond book. The door to our office was locked by a combination device. I always had problems opening the damned thing. The corridor led out into the basement garage, so we were always ready to go.

The downside was that we were nowhere near the Secretary of State's office. That was something of a problem when a madman entered this 'protected' building. He was armed with a machete and a large knife. He was challenged by a security girl I know but refused to co-operate and got through the Northern Ireland Office door. The guys in the basement took off but the knifeman got into Thames House, MI5 HQ, and cut up two security guards. He was brought down by a couple of blasts from a Taser stun gun. He was bundled away and the incident kept reasonably quiet for the breach was a total embarrassment.

John Reid was my first 'active' Northern Ireland Secretary. A tough Glaswegian, with attitude if provoked, he was a staunch supporter of the Celtic football side, and, as my mother came from the other side of the footballing divide, it led to some healthy discussions. He was the first Catholic to be appointed to the position, which suited Sinn Féin president Gerry Adams.

A ceasefire was supposedly in place but it was still tense when we were in the Province. Stormont, the Northern Ireland parliament, had been suspended after the PIRA had planted a spy in rival political offices and this led to direct rule from Westminster. This was a major setback for all concerned.

The situation was ever unpredictable and because of that the NI Office chartered a small jet to ferry the NI Secretary and us back and forth 'over the water'. It sounds very grand but it wasn't; it was small but secure and that was all that mattered. Once we were in Ulster my job was finished: the RUC would assume responsibility for his protection. If he went to Dublin I would take over again.

The SB team stayed at Hillsborough Castle, where we had one of the flats with a good view over the grounds; and watching the changing colours of the trees as the seasons passed was a good distraction from the problems beyond the gates. For, despite the ceasefire, the atmosphere as one travelled around was one of unease. What the general public did not see, or did not care to see, from the mainland was the regular violence, the beatings and worse. This is what the various paramilitary groups called 'good housekeeping', to keep their followers in line. And to send the message that said, 'Whatever you think, we haven't gone away.'

And they hadn't. I was conscious that a Met SB detective would still be a valuable prize for the IRA. I was constantly making sure that we were not being followed. Our drivers were generally retired RUC officers and so knew the Province extremely well, including the no-go areas of West Belfast.

I was given the use of a car to get out of the flat alone. I was briefed that it was safe to go around Hillsborough and Lisburn, but no further. I always told the RUC guards where I was going and how long I would be. They had my mobile-phone number and I had an emergency number to call. I drove up to the gates and, waiting for them to open, was told Gerry Adams was coming into the castle.

Adams was a careful man. He always had a scout car in front of him checking the route was clear; if not, the scout would radio back to Adams and he avoided the area. He was a moving target, even for the IRA, the organisation's hawks, who have long wanted him gone.

Cleaky Clarke, a really nasty piece of work, who is now dead, was the boss of his protection team. He's on film taken from an army helicopter, seen smashing the windscreen of a car from which two soldiers were dragged, stripped naked and shot dead. I always wondered about the phrase 'peace process'.

Gerry Adams had no need to be worried about the security service or the army, for MI5 had spies within his organisation. Nevertheless, they were wily adversaries. As I was waiting, the scout car arrived, blocking the entrance, and a few minutes later Adams arrived sweeping into the grounds like a head of state. The cars pulled to a halt in front of the main door, Gerry went into the Castle and the cars reversed and parked. In full view of the RUC, they started playing with and cleaning their AK-47s.

As they got out of their cars they looked in my direction. The one thing we could not, must not, ever do was underestimate the IRA. They are one of the most effective and disciplined terrorist groups in the world. The same couldn't be said for Loyalist groups. They were a ramshackle bunch more inclined to fight one another than combat the IRA.

I decided against going out and reversed the car back down the slope and parked. As sure as night follows day, there would be more of Gerry's boys out there looking after him and I wasn't going to put myself on offer. I never used that car again: it had been spotted and the car number taken. A 'chance' meeting in some car park somewhere could not be ruled out of the equation, just as when President Clinton just happened to meet Gerry Adams in Mrs Miggins' Tea Shop while out walking on a visit to Ireland.

I couldn't get onto John Reid's wavelength but, as with most of his Cabinet jobs, he wasn't around long. After the supposed tough guy, the Welsh MP Paul Murphy was a breath of fresh air in the post. He had a difficult job, for the peace process was in trouble.

An uneasy calm was policed by paramilitary groups and the RUC, which was now the Police Service of Northern Ireland. After the creation of the PSNI, the uniforms were changed. On their jumpers in gold letters was the word 'Police', on green uniforms with white shirts – the colours of the Irish national flag.

It caused uproar and over time the gold lettering would be changed. This was the tightrope that all ministers had to tread. Ulster wanted to remain part of the Union and any symbolism that detracted from that and to a united Ireland was fiercely resisted. One of the tradeoffs for the peace process was that Dublin removed, after a lot of arm-twisting, from its constitution the phrase 'to be a united Ireland'.

In America, especially in the Irish bars of Boston, New York and Chicago, that, of course, was the Holy Grail. There had to be as much diplomacy as care on visits with the Northern Ireland Secretary to the United States. I went with Paul Murphy to Washington – for the St Patrick's Day celebrations. Gerry Adams and other political leaders were going, too – it was much to do with who had the most clout with President George W Bush.

Under a reciprocal arrangement with the US State

Department, I was allowed to carry my Glock. One other officer was also allowed to be armed. When the Americans come to the UK the same rule applies, but I know that many, many more of their men are armed. Our people ignore it. It must be part of the 'special relationship'. Under certain circumstances there are occasions when foreign officers might carry firearms in the UK.

Yet carrying a gun in another country is fraught with problems. We are given a piece of paper with authorisation, but try telling that to the local police when you get arrested. One SB colleague was stopped and thrown in jail in America and it took forever for embassy officials to get him out. I didn't want this problem. I wanted to go out in advance and check the venues and security.

I was extra careful about the procedure for transporting my firearm, for I'd had a problem with a BMI flight. I had complied with BMI safety instructions and all their regulations. I was told that I could collect my gun at the special-services counter in Belfast City Airport. On arrival I went to the special-services desk, produced my warrant card and asked for my gun. They looked at me with blank expressions. I looked back to the baggage carousel.

All the bags had been claimed apart from a grey tin with a red sticker across it saying firearm. I needed to avoid that sort of nonsense in America.

I flew out four days before Paul Murphy, one day to travel, another to recover, and two days to do the venue security, meet the visit section people at the British Embassy and liaise with the local law-enforcement agencies in Washington, DC. One of the perks on long flights was that we travelled upper class or first and I was in seat 1K on a Virgin Atlantic flight from Heathrow. When I got there a driver took me to the Westin Hotel on Embassy Row.

The British Embassy isn't hard to find: there's a statue of Churchill outside the front door. There, I met up with Bob from the Secret Service. We had an Embassy car with driver Jane to take us around DC. The places to visit were the State Department, White House, Capitol Hill and the Lisle building, which is next to Capitol Hill. We went first to the White House and Bob told us that we should use the rear entrance and not the one always seen on television.

The White House power players are all in the West Wing. This is on the right of the main building in a low, single-storey block of offices containing the Oval Office. I noticed uniformed officers in marked patrol cars. I thought that they were the local cops. They were the Secret Service Uniform Division. Only in America could you have a Secret Service that tells everyone that you are the Secret Service. The main entrance was guarded by the White House guards in different uniforms. It was starting to get confusing. What would this lot make of trade unions and demarcation lines?

Bob was my age, laid-back and friendly, and was helpful with entrances and exits and identity cards for the visit. All I needed was for big Gerry Adams to waltz straight into the White House, which wasn't beyond the realms of possibility given the influence of the Irish lobby, leaving my Secretary of State standing outside. I was assured that it would be all right on the day, yet something was telling me a different story.

We approached Capitol Hill from the left-hand side of the building, turned into the main car park and stopped by a long wide awning – the President goes that way to avoid being seen getting out of the car when a gunman can take a shot at him. The meeting was with Senator Ted Kennedy. The guys doing the security were the Capitol Hill Police. Who was co-ordinating all these different police agencies?

As I was being escorted around by the Secret Service, I received VIP treatment and satisfied myself that security was perfectly in place. On arrival day at Dulles Airport I got everyone together and in four cars we drove in convoy back to the ambassador's residence.

On the steps was Her Majesty's Ambassador to the United States of America, Sir Christopher Meyer, a larger-than-life character. His trademark was that he always wore red socks. He was no lover of the Blair administration. Paul Murphy was his guest, but the rest of the party were staying at my hotel a few minutes' drive away.

We had meetings all over DC, the first with the President in the Oval Office. I went on ahead before the main party with Jane. We met Bob at the rear gates to the White House and he said there would be a slight delay: the names of the people who were due to go inside were not on the list.

It didn't seem a big problem – just give them the names. No, the names had to come from a special department. I said, 'I have the names here; give the guy the names and he can phone whoever he needs to phone to verify the names!'

'Well, that's a good idea but it doesn't work like that. These names really have to come from elsewhere.'

'Don't the Secret Service have any say in this?'

'No, we're dealing with White House security, and they can overrule us.'

This was crazy. Here was a Secret Service agent who knew me and Jane from the embassy and he didn't have any say in the matter. I was to find this out again and again. I had to

Above: Hello sailor! At the *Canberra* the day Lord Sterling announced he wanted to kiss Margaret Thatcher.

Below: My heroine. One of the best people I worked with – tough and fair, which is all you can ask.

Above: Smelling the roses, with Ken Clarke and his wife at his home.

Below: Licensed to… with the squad guarding Clarke.

Salman Rushdie in 1992.

RUSHDIE
IS A FRIEND
OF
SATAN

Publication of *The Satanic Verses* landed Salman with a fatwa from Iran and numerous death threats, entailing round-the-clock protection and live-in arrangements. Here a bomb goes off in a Paddington hotel, killing its maker who was believed to be targeting our man. The threat was serious and real.

Sir Peter Terry, ex-Governor of Gibraltar and in September 1990 the target of an IRA assassination squad which shot him at least nine times through the windows of his Staffordshire home but failed to kill him. I was later to protect the convalescing Sir Terry and his wife at their repaired home.

Above: With Lord Willie Whitelaw at St Andrew's for a day out with the House of Commons and House of Lords golfing societies. Willie was a keen golfer, winning a Blue at Cambridge in the sport.

Below: Farewell to Michael Howard and the Home Office – I was presented with Margaret Thatcher's book *The Downing Street Years*.

Above: A room with a history – while John Major was in talks I had this lavishly appointed area of the Ambassador's residence in Moscow to myself.

Below: Carry on Up the Khyber – the view from my car en route to Taliban territory with Clare Short in tow.

Some of the other great characters I worked with included former PM Ted Heath, the convivial Lord Roy Mason of Barnsley and King Hussein and Queen Noor of Jordan.

deal with the State Department Secret Service, White House police, White House Secret Service, Capitol Hill Police, each with their own set of rules/guidelines. And they stick to them no matter what the situation.

On home turf, if there is a visit from a visiting head of state or senior government official and I'm the PPO, then I take responsibility for all decisions and make it happen. I can order every rank to do as I ask. It is done in a nice way but that is the bottom line in all matters of security. In the States, there is a reluctance for anyone to take this role. The level of bureaucracy was astounding.

The Secretary of State was on his way and no one at this point was going to be allowed in. I told Bob, 'Something has to be done, because the official party are on their way and your President is expecting them. If they don't get to see him and our Tony Blair rings your guy in that building then the "special relationship" will look a bit dodgy, especially as the UK seem to be your only allies.'

As if by magic, the authorisation came through a few minutes before they arrived. The S of S came up to the gates and was given a pass along with the rest of the group. My two colleagues, who were two authorised to carry firearms that day, were getting excited about going into the White House.

No way. They were carrying big guns. I agree with the Americans on that one. We wouldn't allow weapons inside Number 10 Downing Street, and this was no different. I said with a smile, 'Don't worry, guys, I'll go in.' Their faces were a picture. It was of pure disappointment. I took my pass and followed the delegation into the West Wing. The entrance is a double-fronted, Georgian-style glass door. On guard was a Marine in full dress uniform.

He opened the door and we went the main reception area. On the floor was royal-blue deep-pile carpet. The atmosphere was hushed and imposing. Just inside the door was a desk, behind which was the gatekeeper. This lady asked who we were and checked us against her guest list (please let the names be there!). All was in order. At the back of this reception area was the Stars and Stripes protected by another two Marines, one at either side of the flag. Whatever you think of them, the Americans show every respect to their flag and country.

We were escorted to the Oval Office. I waited outside. There were two doors, so no one met the incoming or outgoing visitors. The next meeting was with the Irish Taoiseach (Prime Minister), Bertie Ahern, who would resign that office amid financial controversy in April 2008.

Paul Murphy appeared from the 'exit' door and we were off to the East Wing, where the great and the good of the Irish American community of DC had gathered. I saw Gerry Adams, David Trimble (former First Minister) and other leaders of Northern Ireland political parties. A small military band was playing 'Danny Boy' and other tunes thought appropriate. Instinct kept me ever watchful in this crowd.

Suddenly, a figure appeared on the steps of a marbled staircase that led to one of the other three floors in the building, and announced, 'Ladies and gentleman, the President of the United States of America.'

The band struck up 'Hail to the Chief' and the President arrived in company with Bertie Ahern. The two men stood side by side on the staircase and I thought how powerful the Irish American lobby is in the States. The two men shook hands and back-slapped each other for the Irish television crews and assorted media, and then came down the steps to meet the crowd. It was pure pantomime.

As they went into the crowd with the TV cameras rolling, Adams and Trimble looked as if they were sharp-elbowing everyone around them to get pole position next to Bush. Both men, with fixed grins – as if they'd been embalmed at a happy moment – and almighty determination, pushed and shoved their way through the Irish American faithful.

It worked. There they were next to George W. It was all cheap and tacky, like much of politics. Adams is the master of media manipulation; Trimble loved his own soundbites too.

Gerry and the lads stood back and accepted it all, laughing all the way to the agreement; even ritual killings were deemed by Mo Mowlam, when she was Northern Ireland Secretary in the late 1990s, as not that important. The attitude was that the UK government must not piss off Gerry Adams, otherwise his lot would go back to doing what they do best – and who was going to pay for all the bomb damage?

And this was what it all boiled down to at the White House: a cynical attempt to gain the moral high ground on both sides of the Atlantic, with all involved wanting to be able to say the American President was on their side.

I doubt that the American people give a stuff about Northern Ireland, let alone know where it is. Nearly 90 per cent of Americans do not own a passport and therefore have not been out of their country, and, before he was elected as President, that included George W. Bush.

The charade over, I called the team in. No cars were allowed to drive in front of the White House, so they pulled up outside Riggs Bank next to the Treasury building. As we were walking towards the cars, Adams was giving a TV interview and Murphy was asked if he, too, would say a few words, which he did.

I was thinking of getting a picture of Adams and me shaking hands to see what reaction it would get from Special Branch top brass. I thought better of it.

Chapter Nine
The Queen

'What does a man seek in this world? A position,
or a throne? Man seeks peace of mind and the fear of
Almighty God. As long as one knows that there is a
judgement day he tries to keep his conscience clear
and do what he can.'

King Hussein bin Talal of Jordan (1935–1999)

One of the great charismatic characters I looked after
was the father of modern Jordan, King Hussein, who
was a special favourite of the Special Branch teams. He was
the good guys' good guy. He had an edge, for his family
claimed a direct line of descent from the Islamic prophet
Mohammad.

'We are the family of the prophet and we are the oldest
tribe in the Arab world,' the King said of his Hashemite
ancestry. Yet, with such high connections, he held some
secular views. He didn't like a fuss or people who talked
through platefuls of plums. He called me 'sir'. He enjoyed a
happy relationship with his Special Branch detectives and was
dismayed when he was left in the charge of the royal
protection boys.

Many of them are more royal than the royals. When the
extended Royal Family were downgraded – in protection

terms, of course – this other lot were looking for more to do. As King Hussein had a title as well as being a head of state, the Yard decided his welfare could be given over to the royal squad.

After a couple of visits, King Hussein wrote to the Metropolitan Police Commissioner and requested to have his SB detectives on future visits. We were all delighted. He was highly respected, although a controversial target. He'd helped Jordan through the Cold War and several decades of Israeli–Arab conflict. He was a man of the East who was very comfortable in the West. It was a tricky position, just like Jordan's geographical location.

He was involved with many charities, one of which was Flying Scholarships for the Disabled (FSD). After his death from cancer in 1999, the patronage was taken over by his widow, Queen Noor. She was as liked as her husband. There was no specific death threat against the American-born Queen, but because the late King was held in such high regard the Branch asked me to deal with her protection arrangements for a charity event at the Imperial War Museum at Duxford near Cambridge.

It was a black-tie event in aid of FSD but tied in with another fundraising event. The English aviator Polly Vacher was preparing to fly around the world in her single-engine Piper PA-28 Cherokee Dakota G-FRGN, and this charity event was twinned with this Wings Around the World Challenge. It was going to be a high-flying affair. I had backup from Cambridge SB officers – and I needed them. There were 200 invited guests at £200 a time. It was a sell-out, and much of that was thanks to the attraction of Queen Noor.

I studied the seating plan and found myself a place where I could see the Queen and get to her in an emergency. A worry was that there were exits behind the top table where the Queen would be sitting. I was assured that this was for the catering, and, as this was going to be a low-key event, I let it pass. During a higher-profile event, either this wouldn't happen or, if it did, the door would be guarded in case someone with bad intentions tried it on.

I picked my table and seat, which happened to have three people from the Queen's private staff at it, including Colonel Mohammed from the Royal Guard, the Queen's very own Rottweiler, but thankfully he was on my side. We'd checked out the catering company. The manager knew them all, they would all wear name badges and he had no plan to recruit from an outside agency. But many of the guests were known only by their invitations. The threat assessment I'd received from the Yard desk officer was low. All in all, it was going to be completely routine.

We were going to fly in by helicopter from the Queen's HQ in Buckhurst Park, Virginia Water, Surrey. I asked for a minimal uniform presence as a deterrent. It was police protocol that, because it was Cambridge's patch and I was carrying a gun, the local coppers would be present unless I specifically stated that I didn't want them; given the number of guests, it seemed sensible to have troops on hand.

At Buckhurst Park, one of the guards took me on a tour, down the drive past the paddock packed with polo ponies and into an underground garage. He entered the code into the huge double door, which then slid open and the lights automatically flashed on.

There were thirty cars all lined up and in showroom

condition. It was Jeremy Clarkson heaven, the cream of the crop, all the truly great names were represented: Maserati, Ferrari, Aston Martin, McLaren, Porsche, Rolls-Royce, Bentley, BMW, Mercedes. There were several models of each make.

I'm not a petrol head, but it was an amazing sight to see millions of pounds' worth of vehicles all lined up, fully fuelled and ready to be driven. There was an air-filter system that sucked out all the exhaust fumes as well as any dust, so that the cars remained pristine. The guard saw the look on my face and laughed, 'His Highness loved his cars.'

He told me the King had had a 1936 black Mercedes convertible in perfect condition which he had treasured. Shortly before Hussein's death, the garage foreman tried to start the car, as he did with most of the cars to keep them 'ticking over'. He couldn't get it going, no matter what he tried to do. He called Mercedes UK and asked if there was anyone who could help. Hearing the type of car and the age, they didn't have anyone with that kind of expertise, and referred him to Mercedes in Germany.

He contacted head office in Germany but, when he explained the type of Merc he had, the line went quiet. He was asked again to specify the type of car. Once more, he was asked to hold the line. Next, the head of Mercedes asked him to go through the story again. Immediately the head man said that he would send Wolfgang over to inspect the car and make a report on the problem and how to carry out the repairs.

Three days later Wolfgang, a sprightly man aged about seventy, arrived; the black convertible had been pushed out of its bay for proper inspection. Wolfgang got to work and after a few phone calls back to Germany turned to the garage foreman. 'Do you know what you have got here?' he asked

'No, that's why we called you.'

'This car is only one of four built in 1936. We do not know where the other three are or what happened to them. We thought that this one must have been destroyed. This car was built under the instructions of Hitler. This was one of his personal cars. I have authority to offer you four million pounds sterling for this car now. I can give you a banker's draft within two hours.'

This revelation was given straightaway to the King, who hurried to the garage. He thanked Wolfgang for his trouble but declined the offer. The next day the car was crated and shipped back to Jordan, where I presume it still is.

That day I was brought back to the present by the roar of an incoming helicopter. The pilot Richard, like me in black tie for the charity dinner, waited with me for the Queen. She was accompanied by two of her private staff as well as the colonel from her protection team.

She was stunning, about 5 foot 7 inches and slim. Her blonde hair was tied back and she was wearing an eye-catching, long, midnight-blue, fitted dress.

It was a six-seater Bell helicopter, blue with cream leather seats – all very expensive. We all put headphones on and I heard excited talk coming from the back as to what the evening had in store. Richard went through his preflight checks and slowly the rotors started to turn. The unnerving thing about helicopters is that, before the blades get up to full power, the whole machine rocks until it gets balanced, and that's the part I don't like. Yet in half an hour we were at RAF Duxford.

With the reception and the wine flowing, Queen Noor was

invited to watch a flypast by an RAF Harrier. I joined her and she invited me to sit next to her and watch. Protocol and procedure would be to decline politely, but she was insistent, so I sat down.

Once the main party had assembled outside, the Harrier roared in, doing a low-level pass along the length of the runway. The noise was deafening as it banked over the Cambridgeshire countryside, shattering the peace and calm of the M11. It came back again and made another pass at full speed, a frightening sight. It banked around again and approached at a slower speed and came to a hover over the runway about 200 yards away.

The noise was intense and I had to cover my ears, but the Queen just sat there and took it in her stride. It went up down and turned around and then, facing the marquee, dipped its nose in salute before going backwards, turning and flying off for one more pass – and the magnificent display was over and dinner began.

My table was made up of the Queen's private staff, along with Richard the pilot. Sitting next to me was a big and tall American who introduced himself as John. I shook hands with him and told him my name. He asked what I was doing here and I said I was the co-pilot for the helicopter. At times like that a judgement call has to be made as to how much you tell people about yourself. My natural instinct was to be economical with the truth unless it was blatantly obvious who I was.

The waiters were pouring the wine and my new American friend was enjoying it. The dinner guest on my left was a tall, softly spoken guy. He also asked me who I was and I gave the same reply. He was the driver for Lady Bader, widow of Second World War hero pilot Douglas, who was on the top table.

It was an amiable evening, good company and an easy job.

I kept glancing over at the top table and the people moving about behind the Queen, but this was a low-key affair. There couldn't be any problem, could there?

The American next to me was talking and it was becoming obvious that the drink was beginning to make its mark. 'Are you gay?' he asked. In a diplomatic way I told him no. He assumed that, because I was here on my own, I was. He then said, 'Isn't Queen Noor attractive?'

I looked at him and said that she was.

'I must ask her for a dance later.'

'I don't think that'll be a good idea.'

'She might like to dance with another American.'

I was concerned with his attitude. Was this someone who was fixated with her, just as some people were with Princess Di? Or something more sinister?

Queen Noor's colonel had heard the Yank's remarks and I thought he was going to explode. He was ready to tear the American apart. I now had two problems.

I asked the colonel to stay calm and not do anything, otherwise I would have a major diplomatic incident to deal with. I mapped it out for him. He was a foreign soldier, trying to get hold of another foreigner on UK soil. I would deal with it and he mustn't interfere. The laws in Jordan are somewhat different from those in the UK. I can't take him outside for him never to be seen again.

The colonel agreed to be calm. And then blew it. 'If that man goes anywhere near the Queen, I will kill him. I will kill him.'

He was already looking daggers, if not throwing them, at the American. This was all I needed, an out-of-control Arab ready to kill and die for Queen and country.

The American was getting more animated and belting down the wine. I said to him that he had better slow down on the drink.

'No, I'm OK,' he slurred at me adding, 'She really is something. I must go and ask her for a dance.'

I took out my warrant card and told him who I was and what I was doing here. He couldn't have cared less. He didn't seem to be impressed and continued with his leering at the Queen.

I called over Don, one of the local SB officers guarding the arena, and told him to concentrate on my man. It was difficult for me to see if he was armed. I counted the knives and forks in front of him and in front of the other guests. All were there. It was getting tense and I had to do something quickly, but without causing a fuss. The American got up. I put my feet under my chair ready to stand in a hurry. He walked out towards the washrooms. I looked over to Don and he nodded back. I kept looking at the door, waiting for him to return. It was taking a long time. If Don had arrested him he would have told me. The colonel was alert and agitated and asked, 'Where is that bastard?'

I went over and stood by the Queen. If this guy had given the locals the slip and he wanted to carry out an attack he would come in through the catering doors. I walked up to the door nearest the Queen, and approaching it was our man.

This was enough. Without hesitation I grabbed hold of him, putting my right hand on his throat, forcing his head back, and grabbing his right arm. I pushed him back so that he was off balance and staggering back, all the time pushing his head back. The natural reaction is to grab your throat and try to get the hand off. Doing this, he couldn't reach or take anything out of his pockets. He lost his balance and fell onto the floor. I still had a solid hold of him. The waiters were in a panic but I shouted, 'Police!'

By then Don and his colleagues were there and handcuffed this problem and took him away to their car. I went back inside and no one was any the wiser. I told the colonel that our guest was now in custody and we would not be seeing him again.

'I told you I should have killed him.'

I shivered at that. He meant it.

Moments later, Don was by the door with information. The troublemaker lived in Tallahassee, Florida, and was on holiday. He'd stayed at a local hotel and had paid by a credit card, which he gave. I called up SB in London and asked them to get the FBI to pay a visit to this guy's home, just in case there was more to him. I also asked for a credit-card check.

It took only a few minutes before my mobile rang and I was given all the details about him. There's all the controversy about identity cards but in your pocket and a phone call away are all the details the police will need to find out everything about you – including your collar size if they want to feel it. Big Brother arrived a long time ago, and he's getting bigger and more intrusive by the day.

Back at the reception, the colonel had calmed down and it was clear the Queen was enjoying the evening. I presumed she knew nothing of the incident. Yet, because of it, my guard was up and it was a relief to be back on the copter for the flight back to Virginia Water. As we roared through the evening skies, the Queen looked over at me, 'Tell me, are you gay?'

The colonel and the rest of the passengers thought it

highly amusing. I grinned at her, 'Ma'am I can be anything you want.'

Later, Don reported in that John the Yank was sobering up in the police car, saying it was the drink and he wouldn't cause any more trouble. He'd made to get out of the car but was held back. He still had the handcuffs on and he wasn't going anywhere until the next day, when he was scheduled to fly home. He was taken away to Cambridge cop shop for the night and then escorted to Heathrow and checked off the premises.

When I got back to the Yard on Monday, I was asked to make a full report on the incident. The FBI had raided the apartment but found nothing of concern. Our friend had wangled his invitation via a ticket agency advertised in the local press. You can't take anything for granted.

Queen Noor was one of these people who are a pleasure to work for and with. George Robertson was another. He was the Secretary of State for Scotland when a lone gunman, Thomas Hamilton, murdered sixteen schoolchildren and a teacher at the primary school in Dunblane. The Dunblane tragedy in March 1996 led the UK to introduce some of the strictest gun-control regulations in the world, including a ban on nearly all types of handgun.

As Secretary of State for Scotland, Robertson had to make a statement to the House of Commons on the massacre and the response to it. I watched him speak. He was a man utterly and understandably crushed by these events and on the verge of tears. It was not normal for a politician to be so overcome by events, but this was different. George Robertson lived in Dunblane and his three children attended the school where

Thomas Hamilton had ripped people's lives apart. He also knew Hamilton.

Local people had been concerned with Hamilton's behaviour around people, especially children with whom he seemed to be too close. They did not approve of the way he ran his boys' clubs. With other parents, Robertson had tried in vain to stop the deranged Hamilton's suspect activities. On this day, my heart went out to the families of Dunblane and I too was close to tears. I was a father and my son was the same age as some of the children slain on that awful morning.

Later, in August 1999, George Robertson became Lord Robertson of Port Ellen. The name was taken from a town on the Scottish island of Islay where he was born, and where his father was the sergeant of the local constabulary. He then became the NATO secretary general and from Monday to Friday worked at NATO headquarters in Brussels, returning to his home at weekends. We knew that Robertson had a soft spot for SB protection officers, because his brother used to be one of our colleagues.

George Robertson was one of the most high-profile men in international affairs but for whatever reason he was not given SB protection. Instead, this senior UK political figure, on the world stage, was looked after by his Belgian protection officer – an unarmed close-protection detective, a foreign national doing SB duties. We were astonished and used to complain about it, but then shook our heads in frustration.

Along with everything else, that situation changed following 9/11 and it was ordained that Lord Robertson would now receive armed SB protection when in the UK. On a Friday evening I was called at home and asked if I would do the Robertson protection. As I was between long-term jobs and knowing Robertson's background and his brother, I happily said yes.

My new principal was going to arrive at Glasgow Airport at ten o'clock on Saturday morning. I had to be with him as soon as I could. I scrambled the arrangements and met my SB driver, Dennis, at the Yard at 4.30 a.m. When I got there, Dennis had already checked fuel, oil, windscreen washer and tyres and we were ready to leave the grid.

We went to the sixteenth floor and woke-up the duty officer on the twenty-four-hour desk. Sleepily, he booked out our Glocks and thirty-four rounds of ammunition each. Dennis had alerted our twenty-four-hour office to send a message to all the constabularies that a BMW SB vehicle would be travelling through their force area at unusually excessive speed and because of the nature of our work we were not to be stopped. Any speed-camera reports that we triggered should be sent to SB in London, where they would be quashed.

We left Scotland Yard at 5 a.m. to start our 400-mile journey to Scotland. With our seat belts tight, Dennis said we'd hightail it on the M40, M42, M6 and finally the M74 straight into Glasgow.

It was a hair-raising trip. We made our way onto the A40 at Paddington and Dennis increased the speed. We got through the traffic lights without stopping and after the last set of lights were cleared Dennis put his foot down and took the speed up to about 130 m.p.h. and stayed at that speed, swallowing up the miles.

It was no surprise when we reached Birmingham – roadworks. Dennis slowed the car to about 90 m.p.h., setting off speed cameras as we went through the familiar white-and-red-striped cone area, picking the speed up on the other side.

We passed a police car and Dennis put on the strobe lights in the grill of the car and waved at our colleagues, who acknowledged our presence. Pleasantries over, he floored the car back up to our cruising speed of 130.

The BMW was a diesel, and we needed only one pit stop, which we took near Carlisle. As Dennis was filing the car I took the time to stretch my legs. I offered to drive to give him a rest. The concentration needed to drive at those speeds is immense but not once was I worried about the speed or my or other road users' safety. Dennis was on the ball every mile of the way. He declined my offer and said he was happy to carry on.

The miles passed and so did the time. We arrived at Glasgow Airport at 9.30 a.m. and stopped outside the main entrance. I contacted the local police and the Yard to tell them that the Starship Enterprise had arrived at Glasgow Airport and was waiting for Lord Robertson. He soon appeared and was surprised to see me: 'I didn't expect to see you until this afternoon.'

'We had a good run with no traffic to worry about.'

He had already arranged for his son to collect him, so we followed them at a safe distance.

Dunblane is a genteel part of Scotland and the people are warm and friendly. This protection would require sensitivity, bearing in mind what had happened there. The sight of policemen with guns on the street would open old wounds, which I was not keen to do.

Our routine was that as I approached Robertson's house I would call the armed static guards and they would make ready for our arrival. Later, a more senior officer who joined the team wanted things to change.

He wanted these armed officers to walk to the end of the street and be on patrol for our arrival. I thought that this was unnecessary and insensitive. The family opposite had lost a child in the school shooting and seeing all these guns was bringing back all too painful memories. There are times when you have to put aside what may be good practice for the sake of dealing with local problems. We have to remember the feelings of the local residents and temper the security needs and not alienate the very people who could be our eyes and ears when we're not there. Building good relations with the neighbours is as important as building a relationship with the principal.

The new boy was talked out of his plan but it wasn't all down to me: I had Lord Robertson on side and harmony was restored.

The entire SB team had a good relationship with Lord Robertson and his family, so much so that, when he was honoured by the Queen after he retired from NATO in 2004, he invited us to a reception to mark the occasion. Everything and everyone works better in a co-operative atmosphere. It can also be fun.

One weekend, Lord Robertson was invited onto a nuclear submarine. It was a family day for the submariners and he was to attend with his wife, who didn't like to be 'Lady Robertson'. She'd scowl playfully if I called her anything but Sandra.

I went off to check out security and explained to the naval commander how it would all work. I'd be in charge. He listened patiently and then looked at me with raised voice and eyebrow: 'This is a Royal Navy nuclear submarine. If he's not safe aboard this submarine there's not much hope for anybody.'

Good point, I thought. So I played my joker in the hope that it would make the point: 'Look, all I want is a jolly for the day. I either sit in the car and watch from the shore or you can invite me onto your ship, simple as that.'

'It's a boat!' He looked at Dennis and me and added, 'As there are only two of you, it'll be all right. You can be my guests.'

Robertson had his protection and on a cold Sunday morning we boarded a police launch to take us out to the submarine moored offshore in Holy Loch. The launch was bobbing up and down and the 'driver' had trouble getting alongside. It took a few minutes, but we all got on board to be greeted by the captain and some of his officers.

We had a guided tour of the sub and intriguing, informative talks from the warfare officer. These vessels pack one hell of a punch and I'm glad we have them. I wouldn't want to guess at the full extent of its operational potential but it's not for the faint-hearted.

We were given lunch in the captain's cabin with some of his senior officers and their families. One of these young submariners was extolling the merits of a rather attractive young lady and how he would love a date with her, to put it mildly. I looked, only to find out that I knew the young lady who was the topic of this conversation.

'Yes, she is rather attractive,' I said.

'Absolutely stunning,' was the unanimous reply.

'Would you like an introduction to the secretary general's daughter?'

'You never told us that!

'Don't let the captain know!

'Bloody hell!'

Chapter Ten
The Politician

'The first question which the priest and
the Levite asked was, "If I stop to help this man, what
will happen to me?" But the good Samaritan reversed
the question: "If I do not stop to help this man, what
will happen to him?"'
Martin Luther King Jr, 1965

They'll murder you on the streets of London for fifty quid
or less, so when they put a £10,000 price on the head of
Liberal Democrat MP Simon Hughes the heavy mob were
called in. We didn't want the assignment. A Squad protected
people from terrorists and assassins, not scummy gang bangers.

Yet someone high up in government squeezed the balls of
our commanders and we were on the job – told there was no
one else with the skills to do this difficult protection.

And he deserved it. A democratically elected member of
the British Parliament, MP for North Southwark and
Bermondsey, was under threat of being killed, not by political
terrorists or religious fanatics, but by gangsters within his
own constituency.

It wasn't on. I was first to get the full briefing: intelligence
detailed that Hughes was under a high-risk death threat from
a southeast London gang because he persuaded witnesses to

give evidence about a murder on one of the housing estates on his constituency.

The contract on him was issued immediately after three teenage thugs were jailed for life at the Old Bailey in November 1999 for killing seventeen-year-old Jamie Robe. Drugs gang ringleaders close to the families of the three killers had put up the money. They'd thought their intimidation of potential witnesses to the killing of Jamie on the Osprey estate in Rotherhithe in August 1997 would prevent anyone being convicted. The detectives investigating the murder thought that, too.

Then Simon Hughes stepped in as an 'honest broker' to get witnesses to attend identification parades and give evidence at the trial of Aaron Cole and James Pearce, both aged nineteen, and eighteen-year-old David Huggins, who were all ordered to be detained at Her Majesty's pleasure.

Their gang beat Jamie to death with weapons that included snooker cues and a cricket bat. One crazy jumped up and down on Jamie's head wailing, 'Just want to make sure the bastard's dead.'

Within days of the investigation, police were thwarted by a campaign of witness intimidation, threats and false evidence engineered to stop anyone being brought to trial. Some potential witnesses were warned that if they spoke up they would 'end up like Jamie Robe'.

One witness, Traci Broughton, was only nineteen years old and lost two stone through sheer terror before the trial. The threats were so intense that many witnesses attended the identity parades disguised in balaclavas and boiler suits. At the trial they gave evidence with their identities protected by a screen. A total of nineteen witnesses were moved to new addresses and some were put in the Witness Protection Programme. When the killers were sentenced, their supporters caused uproar in the court, screaming abuse and waving their fists.

In the middle of this was the mild-mannered Simon Hughes, who is a barrister as well as a leading MP. The coppers involved said that without his intervention there would have been no justice for the dead boy and his family.

He'd taken his life in his hands. And he'd done it before, helping a vast number of people over the years at the risk of great trouble and personal danger to himself. When I met him he attempted to shrug off the £10,000 price tag on his life: 'One of my friends said he thought it was offensively cheap.'

Mr Hughes refused to move away from his constituency, but he did accept our advice on most of his security. He held his constituency surgeries inside shops rather than in open malls and we ferried him around southeast London in an armoured Jaguar like past and present prime ministers rather than Liberal Democrat home affairs spokesmen. He admitted of those who wanted his scalp, 'We're dealing with the sort of people who wouldn't find it difficult to get someone to do a shooting or a stabbing for them.'

But he had personal reasons for not looking the other way to protect himself: 'A friend's son was killed and nobody was charged. I saw the trauma that that caused and it made me determined that, if it happened again, we would do better. We must make sure that people are brought to book. Otherwise we're just going to have anarchy.'

The DPG dedicated two armed men to guard his flat, which was a vulnerable setup in Bermondsey. Special Branch had an armed team going everywhere with him. He led a gay lifestyle and he took us everywhere, to all his parties. He invited me into one party in Brockley, in south London. I looked at the entrance and decided that it was safe for him to go in alone. No, he insisted that I go in with him, as there were some people he wanted me to meet.

It wasn't comfortable for me but he genuinely didn't want any of us to be left out in the cold. I thought he was such a brave man, getting on with his life with us present around the clock, witnesses that he was under a death threat.

He kept some strange hours and it was very tiring. After the House of Commons had risen at about 10 p.m. he would go to his constituency office and do some work. It wasn't unusual to drop him off at home at 2 or 3 a.m., go home and be back in to pick him up a 9 a.m.

He had a meeting in the New Kent Road and the cars were waiting outside. It was by the Aylesbury Estate, a place where policemen are not loved. As we waited, someone threw a 5-litre can of red paint over the car with a resounding crash – we got the guns out believing it was the start of an attack. We took up armed positions and I went back into the room where Hughes was holding his meeting, and stood close to him. There was no more action. One young lad told us, 'It was someone having a laugh.'

You must have a required sense of humour to live there.

The MP was constantly busy. He received an invitation to attend the Elephant and Castle Community Centre for a debate about the black teenager Stephen Lawrence, who was murdered in Eltham, southeast London.

In 2008, fifteen years on from the killing, it still resonates. On the anniversary of the racist murder of the eighteen-year-old, there was a memorial service for him at St Martin-in-the-

Fields Church off Trafalgar Square. It was an impressive do, to judge from those in attendance: Prime Minister Gordon Brown, Tory leader David Cameron, Nick Clegg from the Liberal Democrats, Cabinet Ministers and senior policemen. The Archbishop of Canterbury led the prayers and spoke.

It was the work of activists like Simon Hughes which had kept that sad story alive in the public mind. There was no chance he could be talked out of attending the debate at the Elephant and Castle. It was anticipated that more than five hundred people would be there.

From a security angle it was fraught with problems but, despite more urging not to go, he insisted that as the constituency MP he had to be there. Democracy costs time and money.

We had a gangland hit on order and emotions over the death of Stephen Lawrence were at boiling point on both sides of the racial divide, especially in this part of London. I called Carter Street Police Station and asked for a meeting with the chief superintendent to discuss the best way of policing the event.

We decided to split the policing into two main areas. One would be for the crowd control in case the meeting erupted into a riot or public-disorder issue and then would dovetail with protecting Simon Hughes. It would take a lot of co-operation from all the officers involved.

Riot police would be put on standby but out of sight so as not to inflame a delicate situation and be seen as overbearing and provocative. I had been involved in the Brixton riots in the early 1980s and didn't fancy the idea of having petrol bombs thrown at me again. Uniformed officers would be posted on all the entry and exit points so that if anything happened inside, the hall could be quickly sealed off and help brought in.

Simon Hughes would be brought in from a discreet, policed entrance and would be free of any members of the public. Because of the huge number of officers needed, the Commissioner's Reserve and their transit vans – the Yard's not-talked-about 'riot squad' – were brought in to assist. These troops are on permanent standby and can be deployed to wherever they are needed in the Metropolitan Police area.

Our SB cars would be parked at the rear of the building and would also have a uniform presence to guard them in case of trouble.

I had to present this plan to the troops and the senior officers in charge of what was regarded as a high-profile and highly delicate operation. I faced a packed meeting room full of senior ranking officers and me. This was not one of my favourite pastimes but it had to be done. The crowd-control part of the briefing was done by another officer with suitable training, and then it was my turn. I had been introduced as plain 'Ron Evans from Special Branch' at the top of the meeting.

I explained the background and that it was difficult protecting someone from a gangland threat rather than state-sponsored nastiness. The difference is that in the latter case we have the facility to gather intelligence from our spies and sources inside governments and organisations; we had no such information from the criminal fraternity. There were no questions.

It was time to tell Simon Hughes what was going to happen. I was not concerned about that because he was totally on our side, unlike some senior politicians who thought they knew more about protection than we did.

When the story broke in the London *Evening Standard* that he was getting protection, a photographer was waiting outside his home in Bermondsey. The Diplomatic Protection Group, or DPG, who were providing static security outside his house, called me to tell me that 'Scoop' had arrived.

I told Simon that, if we started doing anything to get him away, it would only make the story bigger and give editors a few more column inches. Let's just go home, give him the pictures and he will go away. And that's how it worked. There is no point in a big noise or a big stick when it's not necessary.

We checked and double-checked the venue and the people before I allowed Simon into the meeting. The panel comprised Sir Herman Ousely, chairman of the Commission for Racial Equality; Linda Bellos, the former leader of Lambeth Council; Trevor Phillips, who was then a possible candidate for Mayor of London; and Doreen Lawrence, the outspoken mother of Stephen Lawrence. All the panellists were black, apart from the chief superintendent of police, who was the whipping-boy for the debate.

I sat behind Hughes and observed the proceedings, and, as usual, the police were getting all the criticism, of how racist we all were, and how we didn't help the Lawrence family in bringing the perpetrators to justice. It was all heated stuff from the audience with, in some cases, more measured responses from the panel.

Trevor Phillips, in 2008 the chairman of the new Equality and Human Rights Commission, gave his speech and opinion and then had to excuse himself, as he had another meeting to attend in his campaign to become the mayor. He was saying his farewells to the other members of the panel, but to my absolute astonishment, he walked past the police officer without any acknowledgement of any kind, continued his goodbyes and left.

I said to Simon Hughes, 'That wasn't a clever move.'

He looked at me: 'No it wasn't.'

I was astounded. It was a surprise. There had been no trouble, just good debate, but here we had a man who was running for mayor and part of his remit would be to bring together the police and all communities across London, to break down the barriers and the mistrust that has built up, rightly or wrongly.

It made me even more of an admirer of Simon Hughes. He simply wanted to do the right thing by everybody. We got him safely off the premises and he went to the Commons, back to work.

Chapter Eleven
Cowboys and Cartier

'Go ahead, make my day.'
Clint Eastwood as Harry Callahan, *Sudden Impact* (1983)

L ondon's bad boys are not the only ones who can make life tough on the streets of the capital. The American Secret Service like to play cowboys and Indians in the city and anywhere else they can.

I could never understand why the American protection teams were so uptight. Their track record for assassinations as well as attempts on their presidents is not a good one. They went everywhere in the line of fire with a huge team. Big is not always better. With so many people things are not done in the correct manner and often the assumption is made that someone has done a particular job when, in fact, no one has done it.

Special Branch go around in small, close-working and well-organised teams. This way has proved to be very successful as our 'loss' rate far outweighs that of our American friends. Officially, as I said, two members of their heavyweight teams are allowed to carry firearms, yet the agents, who were never that glad to see us, still bulged in strange places. I estimate that most agents were always packing when they were on duty. Any punk can get a gun on the streets of Britain, and I don't imagine these agents relished being on duty with empty holsters.

Shortly after the first anniversary of 9/11, President George Bush Sr was flying in to watch the Ryder Cup at the Belfry in the English Midlands, and I was chosen to provide protection for him. It was tense enough after the anniversary of the World Trade Center tragedy, and the last thing I needed was Secret Service agents getting gung-ho. I planned to tread gently, but I had to confront the turbulent bureaucratic antics of the Yanks.

There were the American Ambassador's protection team, the Secret Service at the American Embassy in Grosvenor Square and the President's own protection detail from the States. We had to work together. The lead role in much of the operation would be the US Ambassador's protection officers.

The Ambassador to the Court of St James was William Farish III, former president of W S Farish and Company, an investment firm in Houston in the Bush home state of Texas. A former chairman of Churchill Downs Incorporated, home of the Kentucky Derby, he owns Lane's End Farm, a 2,000-acre thoroughbred breeding facility in Versailles, Kentucky, where he hosted the Queen. A special relationship? We'd see.

We comprised a four-man Special Branch unit and we met all the President's men over coffee and cholesterol at a Grosvenor Square conference room. We were outnumbered by the Americans four to one and I thought that this would be hard work.

When a possible assassination target comes to London there are certain protocols that are laid down and are not negotiable. The first is that the SB detective in charge of that person's protection takes the lead role and is the PPO. He will always sit in the front seat of the car and, whatever he says, his instructions are to be followed.

It's no good having a foreigner in charge of protection when they don't know the laws of the land and don't have the authority to get urgent action if there's an emergency. Yet, as the meeting got going, I was not happy and got the impression these Clint Eastwood lookalikes were just going through the motions of co-operation.

They were protecting a former President who was the present President's father. A balls-up wouldn't be good. They were on their toes.

I always got pissed off by the macho attitude – when you shake their hands they will always try to crush yours. It's irritating – and bloody painful. I had to be ready for all the crap that was going to come if their previous behaviour was anything to go by.

The Secret Service want to do everything their way and that can't happen, not because we Brits are being bloody-minded, just that we have different ways of going about our jobs as well as keeping within the law. We have different views on what is acceptable and appropriate in levels of security. The USA is a superpower and the world's policeman but there are times when its arrogance and 'I am an American and I can do what I like' attitude really does piss people off.

We were told that Bush would fly into Stansted Airport in Essex and transfer to a US Marine helicopter to overnight at Farish's home at Winfield House in Regents Park. It once belonged to Woolworth's heiress Barbara 'Poor Little Rich Girl' Hutton and she gave it to the RAF for their use during World War Two. After the war, she returned to see what had happened to her property and it was a mess. She picked up the phone and sold it to the US government for one dollar, and it's been the official residence ever since.

The plan of flying from the arrival and then from venue to venue was perfect. It relieved me of a lot of security headaches and cut down on our already overstretched resources. The itinerary involved the ex-President in opening an American exhibition at the Imperial War Museum at RAF Duxford near Cambridge, returning to Winfield House by helicopter and the next day flying to the Ryder Cup at the Belfry. Nothing could be easier – and, for a golfer, more enjoyable – than watching the Ryder Cup from a VIP seat.

The Duxford opening would be attended by a guard of honour from the US Air Force stationed at RAF Lakenheath and RAF Mildenhall. Also, if it was a good day, the former President would see a flypast by a Grumman TBM Avenger plane, the same type of aircraft he used to fly from an aircraft carrier during World War Two. After the display he would visit another hangar, where he would meet American families based in the UK.

The security details were very easy to put in place. The museum would be closed for the day and all that was needed was for the higher escarpments overlooking the airfield to be patrolled by the local police to make sure no snipers were lying in wait. Jack from the local SB would take care of that detail.

We never travelled on the day of any event because anything might happen – accident, car breaking down or good old-fashioned roadworks – so I stayed overnight at a local hotel. I checked every security detail early next morning and it didn't seem long before I heard the approach of the copter.

After the formalities had been completed the forty-first President of the United States of America was escorted towards the exhibition area. Before we entered, I was introduced to him and Bush was told what my role was. He shook my hand with a firm grip but – and this must be a first for an American – he didn't try to break it. He gave me a warm 'Hi, pleased to meet you.'

And the crowds of US personnel were happy to see him. They roared a welcome. I've been close to other world leaders in similar circumstances and very few of them had this high an approval rating. The applause started to die down and the ex-President started to shake hands with as many people as he could. I'd never seen someone work the line as he did. When people asked about his son, he came out with the same words: 'Thank you very much. He's doing a good job and we're very proud of him.'

The USAF guard of honour started at the bottom of the main path to the exhibition just by an F-16 jet, which was on display. Again, Bush waved and said 'Hi' and the fliers responded. One woman was so overwhelmed that she broke ranks and ran up to him and gave him a big USAF hug. I saw her starting to move but thought better of trying to stop her. I thought, We're among friends here; let it happen. So did the Secret Service.

He laughed and said, 'Well, thank you, how are you?' She gushed that it was 'so good to see you Mr President', regained her composure and returned to her place in the line. He took it in very good spirits and kept on smiling and waving.

It was a good omen for the golf the next day. An armoured American station wagon was already waiting for Bush when I arrived at the Belfry. I introduced myself to the US protection team and looked into the vehicle. Because of my previous knowledge with the Americans I wanted to make sure that I had a place in the front seat, as agreed protocols decreed.

I was told by the Americans that Bush's number-one close-protection officer was on the flight as well. I said that it was not a problem, that we had enough vehicles to accommodate him.

The helicopter landed but it wasn't until it came to a complete stop that the doors opened. A close friend of Farish's had been decapitated by copter blades and the Ambassador would not step out until there was complete silence.

They walked over to the armoured car and the Secret Service guy opened the door for Bush, who got in the back and I thought, Here we go, round one. My concerns were starting to grow, and this was within one minute of President Bush's arrival at the Belfry.

The Secret Service team leader said hello to me and, shaking my hand, he was at the same time getting me out of the way. This is an old society and political trick to 'move' people from your path without appearing rude or insensitive. He smiled all the time and got into the front seat. He was in, I was out.

No way.

I stepped into the front and shoved his backside across the bench seat. There was little room but he couldn't make much of a fuss with Bush in the car; it sounds petty, but once again Uncle Sam had ridden into another country and was trying to have it all his own way. I closed the door and looked my counterpart straight in the eye. After a short while he started to laugh, and so did I. We both knew where we stood and what was acceptable and what was not.

The US Ryder Cup team room was a big conference-style affair, all mirrors and red carpet. Bush went in and I heard him give a rousing pep talk full of what your country expects and how we are right behind you and go and make your country proud and win the Cup for the good of the American nation. And I thought, This is only a golf match. Then I thought again. It's golf, a matter of life and death.

For all the protocol problems, Bush Sr was a joy. He seemed to know all that went on, for he carried a wry smile most of the time. He'd been there many, many times before.

I collect biographies of the people that I have protected. I had one about President Bush, and at Stansted Airport, after he had thanked me for my hard work and for being discreet, I asked him to sign the book. He did so with pleasure and surprise.

I also have Nelson Mandela's *Long Walk to Freedom*. In the early 1990s, before he became President of South Africa, he came to London and I met him off the plane. He shook my hand warmly and thanked me for meeting him, he then introduced his then wife: 'And this is Winnie.'

She shook my hand with a grip like an American secret agent. The smile never left Mandela's face. There was something about this man that I couldn't take my eyes off. He walked with a calm dignity, an inner belief that his time had come. He gave out a warmth and a feeling that you were his best friend and that he had known you for years.

He was in transit in London and I watched over him for

only a couple of days, but he was constantly charming. And, in my business, if you're going to take a bullet for someone, that's always a bonus.

The antithesis of Nelson Mandela was Nawaz Sharif, the former Prime Minister of Pakistan. General Pervez Musharraf ousted him in a 1999 coup d'état and Sharif has been desperate to get back into power ever since. But the general, with his public-school manner and penchant for Savile Row tailoring, has built a strong political foundation. Since 9/11 he has emerged as a mainstay of the War on Terror, claiming to provide the West with a bridgehead into the badlands of Islamic South Asia.

George W Bush and others have hidden any misgivings, and there are many on file. Musharraf's military record shows him as a close ally of the Taliban. Early in his career, he acted as military mentor to Pakistan's home-grown jihadi groups. And no one rebukes him about the terrorists at large in my far-from-favourite spot, the tribal areas of Pakistan's Northwest Frontier Province – probably Osama bin Laden and Taliban leader Mullah Omar among them.

When Musharraf deposed Nawaz Sharif he vowed never to let Benazir Bhutto, the exiled former leader and scion of the country's most famous ruling family, return to Pakistan. Yet events led Ms Bhutto, the first woman PM in an Islamic state, to go back to fight for power. Also looking for his old job back was Sharif.

For him it was a pantomime, and for Bhutto tragic. Only two days after Christmas, 2007, she was assassinated at an election rally in Rawalpindi. Many others died in the attack and several more were injured. And this was in 'friendly' crowds.

I spent a frightening week with Nawaz Sharif who also liked appearing in crowds. He also liked Cartier watches, which he'd buy during tours – security horrors – through the streets of Chelsea and Kensington and, his favourite, Bond Street.

This was an exiled Pakistani politician who spent more in a lunch hour than many do in a year. We'd suggest to him that he might like to look around department stores – try Fenwick or John Lewis. Not a bit of it. His other favourite was Brioni. And we were protecting him while he went shopping. It's a topsy-turvy world.

He had a luxury apartment in Park Lane in Mayfair, where SB posted armed guards. I had to guard him at mass rallies in Manchester and London. It was volatile and chaotic in Manchester. The event organisers didn't, or didn't want to, provide assistance; what stewards there were seemed unaware of their responsibilities or not bothered.

Sharif was guest of honour at the top table. The crowds were pushing the stage long before he entered the building. My colleague Terry and I struggled him to the stage and bookended him. The moment we hit the stage it was pandemonium with the faithful rushing to the font. I just hoped that they were all supporters. The stewards had no control over the crowd and, to my horror, some of the crowd had fought their way to the back of the stage and were behind Sharif. They were thrusting their hands at his face and it was a second before I realised they were pushing paper at him. They wanted autographs.

I rushed to pull them back – any one of them could be a gunman or a suicide bomber – in the only way I could, by force. Sharif looked at me and beamed, 'It's perfectly fine, don't worry. These are my people.'

I certainly hoped they were. Otherwise, we would all go up in smoke. After the speeches, he wanted to leave by walking through the crowd like a messiah. We had no idea what might happen. Terry and I walked with him, trying to push people away. A crowd situation like this is one of the most hazardous scenarios, not only for an attack. There's the constant fear of my gun being exposed and some brave guy grabbing it and using it. But Sharif cheerfully did his walkabout amid that mass of people.

My imagination still plays nightmares about that situation – grim scenarios now horrendously highlighted by what happened to Benazir Bhutto in a 'friendly' crowd.

Chapter Twelve
Secret Service

'I can resist everything except temptation.'
Oscar Wilde, *Lady Windermere's Fan*

It was difficult to resist the special wake-up call provided by some of the staff of a prominent hotel in the west country. It was a favourite Special Branch base when we were in the area with Cabinet ministers or visiting VIPs.

If the duty roster was favourable, instead of the shrill ring of the telephone there would be a discreet knock on the door and the receptionist would appear, snuggle under the bedclothes and perform what is known in courtroom patois as a sexual act. I don't know of any officer who stayed there and didn't book a wake-up in the hope that the more accommodating staff would be on duty the next morning. On a team of four it was not uncommon for the whole team to have close relations with hotel staff. It was the norm and it was rife.

The police have a poor reputation when it comes to successful marriages, and I hold my hands up and say that I am one of those shit statistics. Being out of town too often brings its own pressures, both at home and away. With Special Branch it was even more intense. If you are on a team, usually for a two-year period, every other weekend is spent in a hotel near to the house of the principal. Generally, protection officers spend an equal amount of time away from home as they do at home. Over the weeks and months, friendships are formed with hotel staff or in a favourite restaurant or pub. There's a mystique, a certain fascination, and the image often does more of the chatting up than the man. Hotel staff see you and imagine a James Bond type: a man with a gun, well paid, wearing smart clothes. All taken together, it was a heady mix and many, many of the detectives took full advantage.

When I was on the Rushdie team, one of us, each in turn, used to take an evening or an afternoon off. We had to get out of the house to ease the pressure and stress that we were under, and were allowed to go to our, or someone else's, home for stress relief.

Then there was one officer – I will call him Gary to protect the guilty – who would fall in love with whomever he met. He was working with a high-ranked government minister. As his PPO, Gary went to a conference and met a lady who was representing a private security company at the venue. There was a mutual attraction and over the weeks a friendship was formed.

Gary made the fatal mistake of professing his love in a letter to his sweetheart. The missive was discovered by a quickly jealous and enraged husband. Finding out who Gary was and who he worked for, he pledged revenge and went straight to the *Daily Mirror* and told his story. The *Mirror* phoned the Yard looking for a comment and told our senior officers that they would run the story. They were asked to hold on to it for a time. Security reasons. Amazingly, they agreed.

A detective chief inspector contacted the aggrieved husband and arranged to meet him. He took him to a local pub near to the Yard and got him pissed. This happened time after time. The husband thought he had the Branch over a large gin and tonic or ten. The DCI became his mate and, at an appropriate stage in their friendship, his new mate asked him to withdraw the allegation. The ploy worked but Gary was taken off the minister's team. He was warned to be less romantic, but he couldn't stop himself falling love.

One SB officer had a long affair with a principal's daughter. He was a high-powered politician involved in defence matters but it was his daughter who really kept the troops' morale up. A rather adventurous young lady, she travelled widely.

Clever Carole Caplin, when she was an intimate of Tony and Cherie Blair, was another morale booster. But all tease. When she was hanging about with the Blairs, giving Tony long massages and Cherie tips on style, we had to keep an eye on her – and she knew it. When she'd been working out she'd return to her car in full view of Special Branch and put her kit in the back. To do this she'd bend right over, leaving virtually nothing – and I mean nothing – to the imagination. She'd turn around with a knowing smile and drive off. Her antics were the talk of Scotland Yard. Certain places, such as Bristol, had their own notoriety for sexual adventures. Surprisingly, Barnsley was another. They're meant to be careful with their money in Yorkshire but certain ladies are carefree with their favours. Every Friday the good ladies of Barnsley go from pub to pub looking for entertainment. It's called the 'bunny run' and is a well-known tradition along with short, short skirts and high heels.

Most of the team who were with Lord Mason of Barnsley took full advantage of the delights of the 'bunny run.' A Special Branch detective inspector insisted his driver, Miles, bring him a cup of tea in the morning; it became a huge joke for everybody but Miles. One morning Miles made the tea, and, knowing that his DI had a guest, knocked on the door. It was opened and the DI took the tea. He then asked what the tin was for.

'Oh, it's a can of Chum. For the dog.'

In a nanosecond the door flew open and a very buxom and very irate lady shouted and screamed her disgust at Miles, who was never asked to produce morning tea again.

One-night stands were part of the job and all ranks joined in; no one was safe when we went out of town for the weekend or during the frequent Parliamentary holidays, weeks away. Sex was always on the agenda. I suppose you could call it very safe sex. And not just for us: there are scores of stories concerning members of the Royal Family. It was a popular pastime for our colleagues in royal protection. There were PPOs who had gained the confidence of nobility on the equestrian and Kensington circuits.

Cabinet ministers and government officials also enjoyed close protection, both officially and unofficially. Personal assistants and public-relations girls were the favoured pastime of some senior ministers.

One of the great characters I had crossover concerns with when I was at the Home Office was the Scots gnome-like figure, the late Robin Cook. He had a raging affair with his secretary Gaynor whom – after government intervention – he married. As Foreign Secretary, Cookie received SB protection. He treated his armed guard with disdain. He would go home after a vote or be 'paired', which would allow him the night off from the House. This gave him time to smuggle a 'friend' into his house, which he happily did in full view of the protection team. At times he would go out of the residence, which placed his and others' safety in jeopardy.

Yet we in the protection team thought it was highly amusing, the gnome dangling his rod in the water and getting a nibble. She must have been a game girl and we all wondered what the attraction was. It sometimes seemed like a Greek wedding. The protection team would often have to intervene in their domestic disputes.

The affair was highly charged with huge egos on both sides. The newspapers had the scent of it and, at Heathrow Airport, Blair's mastiff Alastair Campbell issued his cruel ultimatum to the Foreign Secretary: ditch your wife Margaret or your mistress. He held onto Gaynor. After they married it got worse: the SB officers would be forced to quell the temper of the lovebirds.

Cookie and Gaynor were husband and wife after a whirlwind romance, and we know what damage a whirlwind can do. The Blair government thought the same. The awful Alastair Campbell intervened yet again in Cookie's affairs to stop all the column inches getting in the way of Blair being the main story.

Cookie and Gaynor were invited to Highgrove for tea with the Prince of Wales. On the way, Gaynor laddered her tights and demanded that the car stop so that she could buy a new pair, which she did at a local village newsagent. She asked the shopkeeper if she could use his back room to change. Seeing the Foreign Secretary with his armed detective outside, how could he refuse?

Gaynor changed her tights and came out onto the pavement, straightened her legs and asked if her tights were on straight. Hamish the PPO holding the car door open gave her a long look up and down and told her, 'They look OK to me.'

From the back of the car came Cookie's strangulated Edinburgh accent and a loud, 'I think my wife is talking to me.'

Power is the great aphrodisiac – look at the antics of John Major and Edwina Currie; if those two can get it together then the combinations are endless. Major has a PA called Arabella Warburton, who has been with him since he was at Number 10. I was with them in Moscow in May 2003 for a business trip. For three years the former Prime Minister was chairman of the European Advisory Board of the Carlyle Group, a multinational investment firm he described as 'very nice people'. The group's interests were eclectic, from Dunkin' Donuts to the global arms industry. The list of past and future politicians associated with Carlyle, including father-and-son Bush Presidents, understandably provokes talk that such people are there to tighten relationships between the company and world governments.

He went to Moscow on their behalf but had said he had no difficulty with his situation with Carlyle: 'I advised them on what was going on around the world. I would represent them, I would do a whole range of things – but I would not lobby for them, and I did not introduce them to people. That was never my role, and I always made that perfectly clear.'

To me it seemed an interesting company. The Carlyle Group bought ailing companies and split them up. But they'd got me to Moscow, somewhere I'd always been fascinated by.

Before joining Special Branch, I was part of the armed team that provided a motorcycle escort to former Russian President Mikhail Gorbachev. Later, I would be with the now former President (now Prime Minister) Vladimir Putin and Prime Minister Pavlov. From the first, I found the Russians a strange breed. Everyone is suspicious of each other. They are also keen on taking your photo, which will inevitably end up in the file of the FSB, the former and infamous KGB.

Pavlov stayed at the Royal Kensington Garden Hotel in Knightsbridge, where he had a suite; an attractive young lady from the Foreign Office visited before his arrival to make sure that the room was of a satisfactory standard and the flowers were in place.

But the advance party of Russians were already there, sweeping the suite for bugs. Our lady from the Foreign Office was refused entry as the Russians were 'busy'. She didn't seem flustered. Just determined.

The big Soviet spooks spoke to each other in Russian, while the lady from the FO patiently tried to explain in English that the Russian PM was a guest of Her Majesty's Government and it was her duty to make sure that he would be comfortable.

More Russian was spoken in scrambled voices until she'd had enough. In a raised voice, and in perfect Russian, she told them where to get off. The Russian bear suddenly became very cuddly after this brief exchange. She remains a highly regarded MI6 officer.

The evening before John Major's Moscow trip, he attended a reception for the one-time Soviet big man Boris Yeltsin, who offered him a lift on his official jet to Russia. Which was why the next morning we boarded a rust-bucket of a plane.

Major and Arabella went down the back of the plane while went to the front with several FSB operatives. The interior was much like the aircraft: well past its sell-by date. Still, we made it to Moscow. I opened the overhead locker, only to find that my raincoat had been stolen. I looked in other bins and asked the stewardess, but she couldn't speak English. It wasn't a good omen.

We all stayed at the British Ambassador's residence on the Moscow River and opposite the Kremlin. Major spent a lot of time in the residence, so I took the opportunity to look around. Red Square was a five-minute walk across the river. It's on a slope and a steep climb up to the main square. It is dominated by Lenin's tomb, which I went in to see.

Opposite is a very ornate building and an astonishing contrast to what Lenin was supposedly all about. It was a shopping arcade called Gum, housed in a grand nineteenth-century, four-storey arcade on Red Square. Red Square? I could have been on Bond Street or Fifth Avenue in New York. All around were boutiques and the familiar names of Hugo Boss, Dior and Calvin Klein, bars and cafés. Here you can eat like an oligarch, drink like an oligarch and dress yourself like an oligarch.

As I was walking about, taking in the warm sunshine and the culture and atmosphere of a fascinating city, I realised I was being watched. I went into a shopping centre and bought a coffee and a cake and looked to see who was around me. The shops were busy so I had to take time to cautiously pick out who my tail was.

It was a matter of 'dry cleaning', going into shops and looking at clothes or electrical items and coming out of the shop and doubling back on where I had come from. This all had to be done carefully. I didn't want my tail to know that I was aware of him, otherwise it would make it all the more difficult. He would drop out and someone else would take his place and I would have to find the new guy. There would be a team of them and they might change places anyway, but it was all good fun. I didn't believe there was anything sinister, so I took my FSB spies for a very long walk around the city, even though I had no idea of where I was going, but I kept to the vicinity of Red Square.

I saw the tail reflected in a shop window. It was one of the guys from the Yeltsin flight. We were just playing charades: guess who or what I am. It was a waste of energy.

Major hadn't moved from the residence and it was hard to see why he had come. He was due to have a series of meetings during his four days in Russia, but he attended only a few. One of the events was a dinner held inside the Kremlin. Over drinks, a display of Fabergé eggs was exhibited for the guests. I have never seen such stunning craftsmanship and beauty; it really was breathtaking.

Much like Arabella Warburton, who was a fantastic sight in her evening dress. She and her boss looked the perfect couple. Most of the time, John Major and his loyal PA enjoyed the delights of the Ambassador's hospitality and never ventured far from their rooms. Their friendship made it no surprise for me a couple of years later to read a gossip column story:

Is unlikely ladies' man Sir John Major losing his touch?
    The former Prime Minister, who always sat at the plug end of the tub when he shared a bath with mistress Edwina Currie, forgot his manners when he dined out with a female friend the other day.

Exiting from restaurateur Anton Mosimann's overblown Belgravia joint, Major, 62, neglected to open the door of his chauffeur-driven limousine for his companion and instead settled himself into the car's rear seat.

Fortunately there was barely a flicker of concern from the lady herself – but then Arabella Warburton knows Sir John as well as anyone, after Major's wife Dame Norma. A former personal assistant at Downing Street, she was responsible for transforming his sartorial image.

'She has travelled all over the world with him,' says a friend.

She is a striking, statuesque woman. All eyes are on her whenever she enters a room and she has a voice like Margaret Thatcher.

Until Edwina Currie illuminated us all with her diaries, you could wrongly have come to the conclusion that perhaps he had a bit of a thing for Arabella. Certainly in the beauty stakes Arabella wins hands down.

My, my!

Major was a nice guy. I had covered him at Tory conferences and noticed that he was a very tactile man, always touching his female staff, not in an offensive manner but the odd gentle touch on the arm or shoulder. When I meet new principals I always try to find out what their interests are and engage them on that theme. With Major it was easy: cricket. I didn't mention women, too risky, so I stuck to his other passion. I scored a six with that, as the rest of the protection team were not cricket fans.

Nice as he was, I was told by ministers and other insiders that if anything of any importance came up he would form a committee or working group to find the answer. He was always pleasant with me but not in my mind very prime-ministerial. I often heard it said around Westminster that the PM was in Number 10 but the brains were in Hong Kong, a reference to Chris Patten, who'd lost his Parliamentary seat and was then the Governor of Hong Kong.

Major and Tony Blair were friends and had a healthy respect for each other. If you listened to them in the early days of the Blair government, you would realise that they never criticised each other personally, only their policies. Blair was on the phone on a regular basis asking for Major's advice until Campbell got into full swing and spun everything.

Blair was a terrific front man, though it sometimes seemed that the country was controlled by Alastair Campbell and Peter Mandelson. Blair wouldn't sneeze without first asking Campbell and 'Bobby', his pet name for Mandelson.

I was with Bertie Ahern inside Downing Street for one of his many meetings with Blair over the Northern Ireland peace process. Blair, Bertie and Alastair Campbell were saying their goodbyes. Blair was not wearing a jacket and he turned to Campbell. 'Should I put on a jacket?' he asked.

Campbell looked at him as if he was a mannequin: 'No! It looks as if you've been working hard. And it's businesslike.'

I stood there in amazement. The Prime Minister who has led us to war has to ask whether he should put a jacket on. Holy shit! It really was all mouth and no trousers.

Sorry, jacket.

He was certainly a man who, at times, needed a kicking. He got one – at Chequers. On an early visit he played football with local Thames Valley officers and his SB protection team. Being a Newcastle fan and remembering watching Jackie

Milburn play, or maybe not, he fancied himself as a good player. Then again, maybe not. One of our team accidentally gave him a crunching tackle and nearly broke his leg. He was hobbling for some days after that.

It's certainly difficult to know how history will judge Blair. I found both Mr and Mrs Blair to be 'all right' but at times shallow and she seemed, as so often headlined, out for something for nothing.

Even a bed for the night. Despite her anti-royal sympathies she presumably enjoyed the Queen's hospitality at Balmoral some short months before the Blairs' fourth child Leo was born on May 20, 2000. The little lad will find out if he reads his mum's memoir, Speaking for Myself, that it was a cold night in the Scottish castle and she'd left her contraceptive 'equipment' at Number 10 to stop it being unpacked by the royal servants waiting on her.

More relevant to Cherie's subjects was an issue arising when Leo was 18 months old. An article in *The Lancet* had suggested that the MMR (measles, mumps and rubella) vaccine was unsafe and had been linked to autism and bowel disease. This started panic among parents caught in the Catch-22 situation of whether to jab their children with it and potentially endanger them, or leave them at risk from the diseases.

When he was quizzed about the MMR jab in the Commons by MP Julie Kirkbride, Prime Minister Blair said he would not enter into a public discussion about the health of his children. Instead, he expressed confidence in the vaccination, saying that guidelines, which advise parents to inoculate children with the combined MMR vaccine, were sound. Miss Kirkbride said: 'I was disappointed that the Prime Minister did not use the opportunity in the Commons to reinforce public confidence in the vaccine. I can only assume that he has something to hide, which is to say that little Leo has not had his jab.'

The debate still causes controversy. I believe Leo had three separate jabs. When MMR was the talk of the day officers in charge of the Blairs told me what had gone on. I was also told this by a highly and delicately placed principal. Yet it was not an issue Cherie shared clearly with readers of Speaking for Myself, although you might have thought it was one less intimate than what went on in that Balmoral bedroom.

In her book she complained about the attacks by writers in the *Daily Mail* about not being forthright about her youngest son and the MMR jab. She wrote: 'I did get Leo vaccinated, not least because it's irresponsible not to – there's absolutely no doubt that the incidence of diseases goes up if vaccinations go down – and he was given his MMR jab within the recommended timeframe.'

When this appeared in the *Times*' serialisation of the book, the reaction was mixed. One reader posted the comment: 'Ah, but was he given the MMR 3-in-1 jab or were they administered separately? Craftily we are not told either way!'

Indeed, for that was the issue on which the debate turned. For someone who presents herself as a forthright person, this version didn't seem to stack up.

In my view it's a toss-up over who was liked less by those around them – Cherie Blair or Peter Mandelson. Yet, over the years, I've never heard any politician more vilified than 'Bobby'. It seemed everyone in the Labour Party – never mind outside – hated him. Until Blair stood down before he was pushed, Mandelson was still heavily involved in Blair's and the country's decision-making from his EU office in Brussels.

I was told 'Bobby' helped conduct Labour's last general-election campaign from Brussels and Gordon Brown didn't know the half of it. Never did.

One day Bertie Ahern was at Number 10. He also had a engagement at the Institute of Directors in London. We went in for our lunch and Ahern made a speech and answered a few questions. On the way out I was standing by the main door waiting for him to come down the stairs. He was saying his goodbyes, finally stopping in front of me. He said goodbye and shook my hand. I said, 'Thank you, sir, but I'm coming with you.'

'Oh, you're right. Come on, then.'

We walked out into the street in full view of the media with Bertie holding my hand.

He looked at me with a big smile: 'That'll give your bosses in Special Branch something to talk about!'

They already had much to discuss.

Chapter Thirteen
The Baroness

'A handbag?'

Lady Bracknell, *The Importance of Being Earnest* by Oscar Wilde

She was an angel or a devil, depending on your politics. To some she was Margaret Thatcher the Milk Snatcher, or the Poll Tax Demon, but for many she was one of the greatest prime ministers we've ever had. It's not about where your politics lie: it's about being a leader. Today, this country is crying out for someone with foresight and courage to do the things that she did. We have never seen her like since then and I doubt if we will again.

One of the top Special Branch assignments was to be chosen to protect Margaret Thatcher, who even some years after she left Downing Street remains one of the most recognisable figures on the world stage. Almost everyone I worked with loved her. Some more than others.

In November 1990 a bloodless coup took place to oust a sitting prime minister. Margaret Thatcher was coming to the end of her premiership and her inner circle, her kitchen cabinet, were discussing who should tell her that it was all over. In the guarded room was Denis Thatcher, public-relations guru Tim Bell and Sir Gordon Reece, who was known as Mrs Thatcher's Svengali. A former journalist and television producer, he'd worked as her political strategist during the 1979 general election, which saw her get the top job from Labour's James Callaghan.

He'd done much to make her a winner. He softened her image. And her voice: he hired a National Theatre coach to teach her to practise humming exercises in order to lower and deepen her voice. He also advised on clothing, accompanied her to her television and radio interviews and made sure she avoided combative interviewers who would make her strident.

He certainly could help her relax. So what followed at that 1990 meeting was inevitable. The topic of conversation was who was going to tell Margaret that it was all over and that she should stand down as PM. No one wanted to do the job, not even Denis. He avoided the job, cleverly saying it must come from one of the others, as it was a political decision.

'Has to be Gordon,' it was judged and he was given the poisoned chalice. He strongly protested, 'I can't do it! I love the woman!'

'Steady on, Gordon, that's my wife,' said Denis.

Thatcher was only about 5 foot 4 inches tall, but don't forget the handbag – a formidable weapon. The one thing she relied on was loyalty. If you showed her that, then you received it in return by the bucketful. It was not a good idea to try to cover up a mistake. It was always the best policy to tell her of the error. She wouldn't be happy but she would appreciate your honesty and it was better than getting handbagged.

I heard and watched Margaret Thatcher in full fury and it

was a fearsome sight, to be avoided if humanly possible. Yet to her staff she was so generous. Her driver of many years had cataracts in both eyes; Thatcher paid for him to have the operation privately.

She and Denis were inseparable and relied on each other. Denis had his own office, where he would do the home accounts, looking through a magnifying glass. If he saw some expense that was extreme he would shout, 'Bloody hell, Margaret!'

At the end of each day at precisely 6.30 p.m. one of his wife's aides would come down the stairs and tell him that his wife had finished work. He would always murmur, 'About time!' He would go to her office and have a stiff gin and tonic and she would have a Famous Grouse whisky.

They were a grand double act, which is much more than can be said for her twins, Mark and Carol. That wasn't an act from Carol on the TV show *I'm a Celebrity, Get Me Out of Here!* – she's the same in real life. She's her father's double and highly entertaining. In contrast, Mark is just Mark and no one liked him. He was always regarded as a well-off Del Boy.

Luckily, it was his mother I spent most time with. She was a star. After 9/11, all the world's leaders were 'grounded', but not Lady T. She had a speaking engagement in America. She was told that no one of any importance was flying, and that included her.

'I don't think so,' was her reply. The American organisers sent over a private jet for her. She went across the Atlantic and when she flew into American airspace she was escorted by three F-15 fighters all the way to Andrews Air Force Base near Washington, DC. The audience in Washington had not expected her to show up. The ovation went on for nearly half an hour.

She may be older and frailer, but, as far as I'm concerned, she still has more 'balls' than her successors. Especially Gordon Brown. When I was in Washington I'd ask the Visits officials – they make all the arrangements for dignitaries and operators like me – for their ratings of visiting bigwigs. Gordon Brown as Chancellor rated poorly. He also didn't seem to have much of a manner. I gather the Washington crowd thought he was too threatening to need security.

In any case, it certainly says much that a huge percentage of people in an opinion poll in April 2008 said they'd love her back in Downing Street. I fully believed it. Lady Thatcher could stop the traffic. When I went with her to events I was astounded at the number of people who wanted her back in power. It didn't matter where she went.

Lady Thatcher was to attend the final hurrah for the *Canberra*, one of the ships that had been commissioned by her government to transport troops to the Falkland Islands in 1982. The security work for the visit had been completed and I was standing on the dock with Lord Sterling, chairman of P&O. A small group of well wishers were in the quayside as well. Elizabeth Buchanan, in 2008 the private secretary to the Prince of Wales and known around his offices as 'Miss Nannypenny', was there and was talking in depth with Lord Sterling. She'd been a spokeswoman for Lady Thatcher, and a political adviser to Cecil Parkinson and Paul Channon at the Department of Transport. She's an extremely likable person. I also worked with her during the 1997 general election.

At the *Canberra* event she was working for Tim Bell. She

was one of the image makers and was always drafted in to advise Lady T on her outings on the stump. Elizabeth Buchanan was popular with many high-powered figures, and I was told that she was very good at what she did. So, I was surprised to find out in June 2008 that she was leaving her job with Prince Charles after it was reported his wife Camilla was not keen on his unmarried aide's closeness to him. Officially it was said she was departing to run the family farm following the death of her father. She seemed more at home in high society to me.

Lord Sterling got his title in Lady Thatcher's 1990 resignation honours list and was a huge fan. I didn't realise how huge until he approached me and asked if he could kiss Lady T.

'What?'

'Only a small peck on the cheek. To welcome her.'

I looked at Elizabeth Buchanan with an 'is this for real?' expression. The perfect diplomat, she was noncommittal.

I immediately called Gary, the Special Branch officer in the car with the good lady. Gary was fiercely loyal, as we all were, to Lady T.

'Gary, Lord Sterling wants to give Lady Thatcher a welcome kiss. Is that OK?'

'Bloody hell! I'll call you back.'

A few minutes later Gary called and said that it would be OK but added, 'Tell him not to make a meal over it.'

I said to Lord Sterling, 'Yes, that would be fine. But no tongues.'

My attempt at icebreaking humour went down, appropriately I suppose, like the *Titanic*.

Once on board, Lady T and Denis were shown to their

rooms, where they enjoyed a relaxing afternoon before the grand ball in honour of the ship and its contribution to victory in the Falklands. On time, I arrived to escort them.

We were waiting for the lift to the ballroom with the First Sea Lord and Prince Andrew and other members of the social elite. Denis was poking and prodding his ear. The others were looking at him in silence. Lady T asked, 'Denis, what's the matter?'

As with many people who are hard of hearing, his reply was loud. He bellowed, 'Bloody hearing aid! Can't hear a fucking thing!'

'Denis!'

'Sorry, Margaret.'

That evening dragged on and Gary was getting tired, along with the rest of the team, which included one of our Hampshire colleagues. It was about one in the morning and Gary said, 'I've had enough of this, it's past my bedtime.'

The Hampshire guy said, 'I know, but what can we do?'

Gary said, 'Watch this. I'll give her one of my looks and then she'll know I've had enough.'

The local guy laughed and said, 'Yeah, right.'

Moments later Gary looked over at Lady T and gave her the evil eye. 'Now she knows.'

After five minutes or maybe even less she said her farewells to her dinner guests.

Gary smiled. 'You see, she always gets the message when I've had enough.'

Gary was with her for many years; loyalty went both ways. Prior to the 1997 general election Lady T and Sir Denis went to an adoption meeting at her former constituency in Finchley. The meeting was long and boring but afterwards we all went back to the chairman's home for supper and a few drinks.

We were given one of the rooms and invited to help ourselves to some food. In our room we were joined by Denis Thatcher, nursing a large gin and tonic. A bright young man said, 'Sir Denis, come and have something to eat. Man cannot live by gin alone.'

He looked at his glass and said, 'I'll give it a bloody good try.'

The evening dragged on and I was asking Gary what he was doing here. He didn't usually work after dark and I was reminding him that it was way past his bedtime. At that moment the host appeared and said he was looking for another bottle of gin to top up Denis's glass.

'What?' roared Gary. Don't give him any more. We'll never get him home. Give me his glass!'

Taking the glass, Gary soaked a clean napkin with gin and wiped it around the rim. He then put tonic into the glass. 'There, give him that and don't tell him.'

When Gary retired Lady T held a reception in his honour at the Hyde Park Hotel. It was all paid for by Thatcher herself and Gary invited all his present and former colleagues. The speeches were full in their praise and respect for each other.

After the formalities I was talking to other team members and discussing the hot topic of the day, which was a policy in the Metropolitan Police called tenure. This was one of the most idiotic policies ever dreamed up by a commissioner. The basis of this policy was that anyone who had been in a particular department for more than seven years should be transferred to another role.

It meant, in essence, that, in sensitive areas such as Special Branch, once you had done your seven years you could be given a lovely uniform and told to walk the streets. It was crazy. All the expertise and knowledge gained counted for nothing. All the intelligence officers and the handling of informants could be lost, causing damage and playing with the safety not only of Londoners but of the whole country.

We were in full rant mode when we were joined by Lady Thatcher:

'Now, what are you three talking about?' We told her about this tenure. She said, 'Who dreamed up this half-baked policy?'

Standing a few feet away was the architect of the scheme, Sir Paul Condon. Lady Thatcher turned on her heels and walked straight up to the commissioner and started to question him on his breakthrough policy – which never happened.

After the 1997 election the press were camped on her doorstep waiting for her to comment on the Tories' loss of power. I went out onto the street just before Thatcher. She finally came out onto the steps to make a brief statement: 'It was truly dreadful for the Conservatives. I feel sorry for all those Conservatives that have lost their seats, something I never experienced.'

What a star.

Chapter Fourteen
Hello, Sailors

'O wad some Pow'r the giftie gie us
To see oursels as ithers see us!'

Robert Burns, 'To a Louse', 1786

Lady T's nemesis was, of course, Ted Heath. They enjoyed a formidable feud. Or Ted did. He liked to cause trouble. At eighty-seven, he was in poor health and had twenty-four-hour nursing care. And an armed guard. Me.

The threat to him had long gone. Yes, he had brought in internment to fight the IRA when he was in office and had to deal with Bloody Sunday. Towards the end of his life he gave evidence to the inquiry set up by Tony Blair to investigate the 1972 killings in Londonderry.

His testimony worried him greatly. In spite of that there was no threat to him. Special Branch had painstakingly checked his security. It was just a waste of taxpayers' money.

Yet, whenever the security service and Special Branch spoke to him about removing his protection officer, he would immediately call Tony Blair and ask that he intervene. Blair did as he was asked. He ordered that Ted Heath be protected until his death. And so it was, until, aged eighty-nine, Heath died in July 2005.

I was not impressed by the news that I was to look after Ted Heath. His reputation of being curmudgeonly, moody and sulky was well known. It also looked like a tiresome job but it was to be most educational. I was told that, if I did this assignment up to the next election, I would be moved onto the Foreign Secretary's team as a thank-you.

With this carrot dangling in front of me, I went down to Salisbury. I would stay there for a week at a time, change over with another colleague at the end of the week and so on. I found a room above a bar in the centre of the town. It was comfortable and within walking distance to Ted's mansion.

Sir Edward lived in a magnificent Queen Anne house in Salisbury Cathedral's grounds, which were simply beautiful, with carefully preserved lawns and wonderful flowers in the summer. Inside the house it was no less impressive. Just inside the door was a vestibule, where all his sailing memorabilia was displayed.

The glass cabinets were illuminated in the evening, as Sir Edward liked to see them when he came home. On the left was his music room with a baby grand piano. Photographs on the piano from his time as PM showed him with Chairman Mao, Leonid Brezhnev and many others. There were also pictures of his mother and family from Broadstairs in Kent, where he was born and brought up.

Further along the hall on the right was another room, which contained his music collection. It was almost floor-to-ceiling CDs, and they were all catalogued. On the right was the kitchen, which had a large table in the middle where his staff would have their meals.

Ted had a small staff: a personal assistant, a housekeeper and a gardener, as well as his nurse and me. His staff was supplied with food from his accounts, but the nurses had to provide their own. Ted kept a tight rein on his money and checked his accounts regularly.

The stairs had a chairlift and the walls were decorated with hand-painted Chinese artwork, which cost £250 pounds a roll in 1986 real money. He liked all things Oriental and as PM he went to China. When I was with him I became aware that he had a boyfriend who would call him from time to time. One day he told me that, when Ted died, 'all this will be mine'. But Ted loved him.

At the top of the stairs was Ted's office with bathroom attached and next to it was his bedroom, which overlooked the cloisters. He slept in a large reclining chair. This is because one night he got so drunk that he fell out of bed. He blamed the bed and not the Scotch for his fall, and a Parker Knoll bed was bought for him to sleep in. He would go to bed very late and get up late, too.

On the other side of the hall were two bedrooms, one for his nurse and the other for his housekeeper.

I found it very strange, for we all know that he didn't like Margaret Thatcher but he clearly hated all women. He could be unbelievably rude to the housekeeper and his nurse. It was embarrassing to be around. He didn't care whom he upset.

When I first met him he was sitting in his office in another of his reclining chairs. He was a large man and the ravages of drink and poor health had taken their toll. But the Grocer's Grin was there and he welcomed me into his home. We exchanged pleasantries and he told me that he wanted to go out that evening for some supper, as it was his housekeeper's day off. It became a routine.

While I was with him he never once called anyone by name. We were 'my housekeeper', 'my nurse', 'my police officer'.

He liked to go out to dinner about a thirty-minute drive from home so he could work up an appetite looking at the countryside. I turned up at the house at 7 p.m. along with his official car driven by long-suffering Colin. He had been with Ted for many years. On one occasion someone asked Colin if he was Ted's son. A very indignant Colin said 'No!' but they were similar in size.

Ted would come down the stairs on his chairlift. At the bottom I would be waiting with his wheelchair. He would get off the lift, into his chair and I would have to push him to the front door, where Colin would be waiting. He would then help him down the few steps and into the front seat of the car. The nurse and I would sit in the back. We would then drive to whatever eatery he had chosen.

Once there it would be up to Colin to get him out of the car, which was a magnificent sight: two bull elephants pushing and grunting together. When he was out of the car he would adjust his coat and then it would be my turn.

As I would have to eat with him I would have to take him into the pub. I would have to put my arms around him, because that's what he liked, and hold him steady by holding his hand. We would then go to the door of the pub and with it wide open he would announce his presence: 'Good evening.'

He was well known at all of these pubs and restaurants and the owners would make him welcome. However, standing at the door with my arms around a gay man was not my idea of fun or protection. He said to me he wanted us to be seen as a couple. He certainly liked to be held. Once we had eaten, we would make our way back home and I would take him back upstairs to his office.

This ritual would happen 363 days of the year – Christmas Day and New Year's Eve off – with whichever Special Branch officer was assigned.

I know it was silly but I got a little precious about it. Yes, I did find it very embarrassing and demeaning doing this protection; I felt I should be doing more important assignments. It was an overindulgence of an old man and should have been stopped and the protection removed. Protection officers were thin on the ground after 9/11 and to have two men to look after Ted was a waste of resources and finances.

Ted wanted to go on holiday and he chose Gran Canaria. My colleague went on ahead, at taxpayers' expense, to do the recce in the sunshine and speak to the British Consul to assist him in making 'security' arrangements.

Before the holiday he had sacked his regular nurse and found another. She was very capable but, because of his dislike of women, it caused problems right from the start. It ended when I had to tell the poor girl that she was sacked and she was to fly home.

This wasn't my job but I got stuck right in the middle of it. She decided to sue Ted for unfair dismissal and other charges. I was named in her allegations. I reported all this back to the Yard but it was very much a case of 'do the best you can'. They didn't want to know. Happily, the situation walked away from me.

The Consul found a nurse on the island who was a friend of his. She was also subjected to Ted's tantrums. I made the bad mistake of suggesting a male nurse; he must have liked me because my comment was ignored. Most days I had to sit with him and look out from his room over the sea, and in the evening take him out for a drive using local taxis. Back at the hotel I would push him in his wheelchair around the large bar area. He loved to be recognised and, if he was, he was delighted. It made his day.

One evening he decided to have an after-dinner drink at a bar. I found a table and brought him the drinks menu. He was by now off the hard stuff. He chose a non-alcoholic piña colada and his nurse had the same. I had a small beer. I ordered the drinks and they were brought to our table. Ted took a sip and said, 'Hmm, very good.'

The nurse put it to her lips and said it had alcohol in. By this time Ted was halfway through his drink and had asked for another one. He was getting very chatty indeed. He even spoke to the nurse. I took him to his room much later than normal, as he had been the life and soul of the bar. I'd never seen him happier, and never did again. I only hoped he didn't wake up with a hangover.

Ted Heath wasn't the only sailor I met. I had to escort John Prescott back to his constituency home in Hull. I arrived at the office of the Deputy Prime Minister and went into the main office.

I briefly met Tracy Temple, his girl Friday, and, as we later found out, on other weekdays too. She was a very nice girl, chatty and friendly, and what happened to her was a shame.

The big man, Prezza, appeared and was jovial enough. We were off to Hull in one of his two Jaguars. We had just got on the way when Prescott started to tell me all about the egg-throwing incident during the 2001 election. Craig Evans, taking part in a countryside protest, had chucked an egg at Prescott as he walked into an election meeting in Rhyl, in North Wales. In retaliation, the Deputy Prime Minister had punched Evans on the jaw with a swinging left hook. In the car, Prescott was clearly proud of himself. Yet he kept pointing out that the newspapers failed to say that some yob had attacked a sixty-year-old man.

We stopped at a motorway service station as we both needed a comfort break. We went into the gents' and of course everyone recognised him. I'd been warned about his temper: he'd been known to pick a fight with members of the public who called out to him.

I think that the protection officers with him were for the public – to keep Prescott away from them. He was the liability, as he was very thin-skinned. I went to the usual place and he went into a cubicle. At the time I thought that he was shy and didn't want to stand percy to percy. Maybe he was going to throw up, have one of his bulimic attacks. But he was an awfully fat man for someone with an eating disorder.

Thankfully he listened to his music most of the way and I didn't hear any more tales of his heroism on the campaign trail. I got him home, checked security, and his wife Pauline was there to greet him. Happy families, indeed.

Chapter Fifteen
A Fair Cop?

'To be honest, as this world goes / Is to be one
man picked out of ten thousand'
William Shakespeare, *Hamlet*

Happy families? It can change in an instant. September 28th will always be engraved in my mind. The first is that it is my wife's birthday, and the second is that it in 2003 it brought me the biggest turmoil in my family's life.

It was a Wednesday and I was in Salisbury, packing to go home after spending the week standing armed guard over Ted Heath. It was just before seven in the morning and I had packed my clothes and put my gun into my bag. I was going to get the 7.30 train from Salisbury to Waterloo. The PPO who was going to relieve me would arrive at about 2 p.m. and as Ted would be asleep, it was common practice for whoever was in Salisbury to leave early.

I was thinking of getting flowers for my wife and picking my sons up from school, when there was a knock on the door. I opened it, to be confronted by three men, one of whom was a DS from the Branch.

They abruptly told me they were investigating me for fraudulently claiming expenses that I was not entitled to claim, and I was cautioned not to say anything and that whatever I say etc, etc.

I sat down in complete shock as the investigating team went through my bags searching for evidence. The DI asked me if there was anything at my home address that would help them with their enquiries. There was a team waiting to raid my house.

I knew at this time that my wife was up and getting ready for work and about to take my boys to the child minder. Fear now gripped me.

The thought of these officers raiding my home with my children inside was too much to bear. I had never felt so low and vulnerable. I assured the DI that there was nothing of interest at my home. Thankfully he believed me and called the officers sitting outside my home not to go into it. It was a small comfort compared to what I was about to face for the next 18 months.

At that moment I was alone and with my mind in overdrive.

Remember, I'm a career copper.

With the search of my belongings over I was escorted down to the waiting police car to be escorted back to London, and into Hounslow police station. Panicking, I asked what was now going to happen. I was told by the DS that I would be taken back for questioning.

The journey took forever. I was now thinking of my wife and children and of course the consequences and repercussions of what I had done.

During the journey my life flashed before me – what had happened over the years, and the culture in this 'old boy's network.'

By the time I joined SB and first went out of town I witnessed the corruption that went on from all ranks. Buying alcohol, meals for wives and girlfriends, was the norm. I stood next to a respected DS as, with a waitress, he wrote out receipts to cover our drinks bill. I was aware of it when I was protecting Salman Rushdie and knew it was wrong.

Don't misunderstand me, I knew what all of us were doing was wrong and in those early days I knew that this shouldn't be happening and I should say something about it. But it was so endemic and, being a very junior officer, having just joined one of the most specialist departments in any police force, I kept quiet.

I was so ashamed – I still am – over my actions and will always carry the stigma. However, in my naivety I thought that because so many other officers were swimming in the same pool as me, all that would happen was that the job would ask me to resign and go quietly, which I would have done. After all, this wasn't such an unusual crime: there are many institutions where employees claim a few extra miles on their allowance or claim for a meal which they're not entitled to.

We couldn't claim for drinks we bought for our principals but it was done, and the only way to 'get the money back' was to inflate the price on a meal or claim an extra taxi ride to offset our expenses in carrying out our duties. But it was wrong and now it was time to pay the price.

We arrived at Hounslow police station and I was taken into the custody suite and the facts were related to the desk sergeant. I was now a common criminal, just another statistic. I turned out my pockets and my money was counted and possessions itemised, including my warrant card which was placed on the desk. The sergeant asked me to sign against the list and said that I could put my personal items back into my pocket, except for my mini Filofax with my credit cards which was kept as part of the investigation. I argued that all my phone numbers and bank cards were in the wallet but it made no difference, it was sealed in a bag. It was then discussed whether I should be placed into a cell. The final ignominy. My world, my career, one that I had given so much time and effort to, had come down to this. The fall from grace was swift and merciless.

I was not placed in a cell but allowed to sit in the main charge room to wait for the duty solicitor to arrive before the questioning could begin. My 'friend' from SB was waiting to offer me his help until the Federation Representative arrived to assist on the 'welfare' front. Nevertheless, I felt I had been cast adrift, hung out to dry, the sacrificial lamb.

The duty solicitor from the Federation arrived and the interview began. Receipts were shown to me and I was asked for an explanation and a reason for them. I had none. I was guilty and there was no reasonable explanation. I answered all the questions truthfully, as I did with all questions that the DS put to me.

The interrogation was dragging on and time was getting close to the time where I would be late in collecting my children from school. After a week away they are always excited to find me waiting for them and would run up to me and give me a big hug. Today would be a disappointment for them. I wouldn't be there.

The interview stopped so that I could arrange for our child minder to fill the gap and make them their tea, as I didn't know how long I would be. I still didn't have the courage to ring my wife and tell her, not on her birthday.

During this break I had an opportunity to speak to my Federation Rep. There was no way out of it – I was guilty and all I could do was fully co-operate in the hope of coming out of this with some self-esteem. I had some kind of romantic notion that if I resigned from the police they would stop the investigation. It was only an internal investigation and I thought it could be dealt with internally.

I asked the Fed Rep to call the Deputy Assistant Commissioner for Specialist Operations which covers SB and ask him if he would accept my resignation. He called Andy Hayman's office, the same Andy Hayman who sat next to the Commissioner of the Met during the de Menezes shooting in Stockwell, the same Andy Hayman who retired in December 2007. Hayman said then that despite being only 48 years old and the Met's most senior counter-terrorist policeman, 'the time was right' for him to go. He said he had faced 'hurtful and unfounded' accusations, which included a row over allegations that he was cavalier with his expenses claims totalling £15,000. On 5 December 2007, the *Daily Telegraph* reported that his supporters claimed that Hayman was a victim of 'dirty tricks'. Allegations were repeated in the media, which Hayman denied.

I am not trying to lessen my crime; all I am doing is highlighting the depth of the problem. I was investigated for 18 months over £400. Hayman went relatively quietly with a full pension but this was not the case for me. Hayman accepted my resignation and I was to go to the Yard the next day to sign the necessary paperwork.

I asked my solicitor about implicating other officers when I was shown my expense claim form, a 287. The other officers that I worked with were doing the same as me, often with me.

She told me that this was a legitimate tactic and that I should do it. But I wasn't comfortable with it. I still had some kind of misplaced loyalty to my now former colleagues. Why should I put them through the same wringer as me? However, I named other officers, since they were mentioned on my 287 expense form. I told the DS about what I knew of the practice, and that these other officers also knew what was happening.

The interview went on and on without respite. It was now early evening; my wife would be on her way home and still I had not spoken to her. That evening, apart from planning on going out for dinner, we had been due to go to and visit a local school for my eldest son who was leaving his junior school. I couldn't make either, and to make things worse my wife was trying to find me and calling me without response. Eventually I was allowed to call her and tell her that I had been caught up at work and I would be home as soon as I could. Needless to say she wasn't happy but what else could I do?

I'd been nicked.

At about 8 p.m. I was bailed to return to Hounslow police station for further questioning. A fellow officer, Neil, took me home. I have to say his kindness was a pleasant surprise and he did his best to cheer me up. He dropped me off and I thanked him. I never heard from him again. In fact I never heard from any of my former SB colleagues again. I was persona non grata. The only colleagues who contacted me were from my days in traffic patrol 14 years earlier. And it was their friendship that literally kept me alive. On several occasions I had considered suicide and actually planned it. I couldn't take the shame anymore. It was affecting my marriage, my children. I could no longer look my family in the eye. I was not eating or sleeping.

I went through the front door to my home and now had to face my wife. She was not happy, not about missing her birthday but once again putting my job before my family. I let her harangue me but she could see something more serious was wrong. She stopped talking. I remained silent for what seemed an eternity. I couldn't find the right words to tell her. I was speechless.

There was nothing I could do except blurt it out. She looked stunned, shocked and then burst into tears. My shame was getting worse. She went into another room and stayed in the kitchen, silent. I looked around me, surveying the instant wreckage of our lives. From that very moment nothing would be the same again. I sat there unable to think, let alone talk. She went to bed and at about 2 a.m. I went up too, but I just lay awake, feeling utterly empty. Twenty seven years down the drain and it was entirely my own fault. No-one else to blame except me.

The next morning I tried to remain cheerful for my two sons. They went to school and I went to the Yard to hand in my resignation. I arrived at 10 a.m. and was escorted to the chief's office. I was scared and nervous and signed everything that was put in front of me. I soon left, plain old Ron Evans.

I went back home and thought carefully about my next move. I needed money. I went into the local employment agency and found a job delivering chocolates in London. I had to drive from the factory in Tunbridge Wells and deliver chocolates to Harrods and hotels for £300 pounds a week. It wasn't enough but it helped. I asked my mother to help and for the next few months she paid our mortgage. She never knew what had happened to me and thankfully she never will.

I was getting steadily deeper into debt and my depression

was getting worse. I refused to go to the doctor for treatment but my wife had to. She was feeling it more than me, but I didn't see that – I was now wallowing in my own self-pity and I couldn't break out of it.

It was time to go back to Hounslow for another interview. I had a new legal team but I just wanted to get the nightmare over with. I would have said anything just to bring it to a close.

Before the interview began, the DS told me that the investigation would be centred on England. Then, the investigation was narrowed to my time in Salisbury when I protected Ted Heath and I had to pay for most things then try to get the money from Ted. Fat chance. The Heath assignment was a one-man protection – the only time I had worked alone. This meant that I couldn't involve anyone else – they were out to get me and me alone.

I was seething with rage. But I played the game, all the time trying to keep my dignity, or what I had left of it. The DS then asked me about my 'holiday' with Ted on Gran Canaria. Now I could fight back. I had paid for everything on this holiday. I took taxi rides to do recces, etc., on several occasions Ted came with me. If he did then he must pay. Like hell did he. At the time I had called the Yard and explained my predicament. I was told to get my money from him and do the best I could. I had been running out of money, paying for all his meals and expenses, so to cover my costs I did what everyone had done in the past and inflate a few bills to get back only what was owed to me. When I had returned to London I submitted a full report to Ted's file. I could tell the DS this and implicate others. I told him that I would only answer questions on Gran Canaria once he had read the file.

I was never asked about Gran Canaria again. All the time

all they were trying to do was get me, and get me they did.

I was still working delivery with my chocolates as a white van man. This job was a real eye-opener. I would walk into shops and because I was only a driver the attitude from some of the shopkeepers was rude and arrogant in the extreme. It was a valuable lesson in life; lessons like these I was learning every day. Without the comfort of my warrant card, I felt naked. It was a strange feeling, making my way in the world without it. From travelling the world in a privileged position to being a van driver was a reality check.

On the night that Liverpool played Inter Milan and won on penalties I was facing my own drama. That was the night I was formally charged and bailed to appear at Feltham court to answer for my crimes.

I appeared at Feltham magistrates court for the hearing. I glanced around the court looking for any cub reporters who could be seeking a scoop. Luckily there was none. I hoped that I would be dealt with at this court but they refused jurisdiction and referred the case to the Crown Court.

The prosecuting solicitor was really gunning for me and from that first appearance I had my first dread of going to prison. It all seemed to be heading that way, and I was getting really scared. A police officer in prison is not a good idea. They have to be segregated and protected. I was still on the downward spiral with no sign of stopping.

On the morning of the Crown Court hearing, I said goodbye to my wife and children. I didn't take any other clothes; I wanted to remain positive and focus on coming back later in the day and avoiding prison. My wife asked if I wanted her to come but I said no, I would do it alone.

My QC was also giving me warning signs, telling me how

he was going to try to get the sentence reduced. Fucking hell! The nightmare was almost complete. How would I explain to my children, to my mother, that I would be serving at Her Majesty's Pleasure rather than on Her Majesty's Service?

I stood in the dock behind shatter-proof glass and listened to the prosecution tell the judge the facts of the case. I had already pleaded guilty and hoped that my conduct throughout the investigation would help my cause.

It was not going well. Listening to this catalogue of what a no-good son of a bitch I was, I would be lucky to get away with hanging. I was now resigned to going inside; there was no way out of it. My QC started his reply, but the judge kept stopping him saying 'Yes, I know all this.' I looked over to my QC and pleaded, 'Say something good.' He had previously asked my for any letters of thanks from the various people I had looked after. I did have such letters but from a few years ago. However, I had approached people who might offer some support. These letters were passed to the judge and he looked at them only briefly.

My QC sat down, and the judge asked what the prosecution costs were. My QC looked over at me and I looked back. If I was going to prison then there would be no costs. The prosecution gave the figure. The judge stopped writing and looked at me. I stood up, my legs like jelly, as the judge addressed me. He said that it gave him no pleasure to have someone like me standing in front of him. My breath became short and I felt faint.

Then it happened. He said he would not impose a prison sentence but instead I would be fined £6,200. My knees buckled. I cannot describe my emotions. I had escaped prison and been fined. He asked me how I wanted to pay. I asked for

14 days and he agreed. Case closed. I looked over at my interrogators, who looked very disappointed. I don't know how I walked out of the court, but the relief was immense. When my solicitor found out all he said was 'Staggering.' And it was.

I paid the money by virtue of a kind friend. I had no money, no savings, only a huge debt.

The job also tried to confiscate my small pension but was stopped from doing so by my legal team.

I now had to pick myself up. I felt as if a huge weight had been removed from my shoulders, but I also felt a great anger at what had happened to me over £400.

I admit I did wrong. I was in a position of trust and I betrayed that trust and paid the price. I have not named all those officers who were with me and who made fraudulent claims. I feel anger over some of my sanctimonious colleagues who say they had never made similar claims. I will keep my own counsel and take all the bricks that are going to be thrown at me and I will not throw any back, but I know what goes on.

I still bear the shame and the stigma of that episode and yes, it still hurts. But I take pride since then that I have built a new career, found a new job and kept a roof over my children's heads, although I am no longer married and I live alone.

I have left those dark days behind me and have come out a better person. I still do my job, the same job at heart – keeping people alive and out of trouble.

Chapter Sixteen
Gun Smoke

'Whatever you do, don't let him get to the Tube.'
Metropolitan Police Commander Cressida Dick, 22 July 2005

I was taught to kill but not to murder. It's a fine line. When bombs started going off in the streets of London in the summer of 2005 I had left Special Branch and had become a gun for hire.

I was working in Saudi Arabia and it was intriguing to see the reaction from there coupled with my inside knowledge of the split-second judgements involved in what became a cavalcade of blunders and contradictions.

I had known – we'd all known – that, following the horror of New York, it was only a matter of time before London would be targeted for something similar. The UK's standing shoulder-to-shoulder with the USA was a gilt-edged invitation to terror. Bush played us, and most especially Tony Blair, for a patsy. What could we offer other than blind allegiance? The UK is not a superpower; our brave troops are poorly equipped and at full stretch worldwide.

I knew that the security services had disrupted many earlier attempts to cause havoc throughout Britain, so the events of 7/7 were of little surprise. The problem for the Anti-Terrorist Branch and MI5 was that they didn't have enough boots on the ground – either in the number of surveillance teams or case officers to follow up suspects.

The Metropolitan Police's Specialist Operations were and are handcuffed by lack of manpower and the ever-clanking chains of political correctness. It was acknowledged throughout Special Branch and in all areas of intelligence that it was almost 100 per cent certain that any atrocity carried out in the UK would be by home-grown terrorists: the boys next door, the nice neighbours who 'always kept themselves to themselves', always said 'good morning' if you did meet them, were polite, helpful to old ladies crossing the road.

And, behind the curtains, mad bombers.

There were plenty of those to go around, yet we had the liberal elite screaming about human rights just as loudly as Islamic clerics were promoting death and destruction to the nonbelievers.

Civil rights and freedom at times of such attacks do not go hand in hand. Prime Minister Tony Blair said at a news conference that the rules had changed and that the government was going to get tough. It never happened in my day. With panic setting in from the government and the overstretched security services, something was bound to go wrong.

Throughout my training, whenever the subject of suicide bombers came up, the talk was always heated. I could use only 'reasonable force' to deal with any situation. There've been high-profile cases where people have been convicted of using excessive force: soldier Lee Clegg in Northern Ireland and farmer Tony Martin in Norfolk.

The police are no different. Be you ever so high, you are not above the law. The test was that I must have an honestly held belief that I was in immediate fear of being blown up or shot and that the only way to prevent that murder was to use ultimate force.

I was given, and trained to use, a pepper spray and a gun. In the event of an attack I had to decide which weapon to counter with. I was told that if I used a gun when the pepper spray might have sufficed I would be charged with manslaughter or even murder. That was and is the dilemma facing all armed officers every moment they're on duty. Instant decisions have profound effects on all those involved.

Throughout all the years, I never carried a pepper spray, always and only a gun. During training I was asked what I would do if a man was coming at me with a knife? I said, 'I would shoot the bastard.'

This was not what the trainers wanted to hear. I was told that I had to make a choice of weapon. I told them, 'I would rather be tried by twelve men in a jury box than carried out by six in a coffin.'

It's like the suicide watch at the House of Commons, always, always, risky.

How do you spot a traditional suicide bomber? He or she and, more and more common, pregnant women or women with babies in their arms will be wearing a thick jacket or a large coat to conceal the bomb. The deadly device would be made up of high explosives packed with nails or ball bearings, created to cause the maximum death and destruction.

Hanging from the bomber's neck would be a thick metal

plate with the bomb placed against it. At the moment of detonation the blast goes out, away from the body so that less of the energy is absorbed and 'wasted' on the bomber, and the victims are hit by the full impact. The bomber is nearly always drugged, so they don't have second thoughts but have a 'happy feeling' about going to heaven to meet their virgins.

When I went to the Commons to try to pick out probable bombers, I went there unarmed and dressed like a tourist: check shirt and camera. As I explained earlier, if I spotted a bomber, then I would identify him to information room at Scotland Yard and a senior officer would make the decision for a sniper on the roof of the Treasury building to kill him. This was Operation Kratos, our shoot-to-kill policy.

Given such circumstances, the police were judge, jury and executioner, all in the space of a few moments. In those early days, if a police officer shot the wrong man then the families would sue the commissioner, which meant the Metropolitan Police, the institution. That has changed and it is now an individual responsibility, and so the officer who fired the shot is sued. Yet, when a senior officer is operating from an information room away from the scene of conflict and giving the order to kill someone, how can the circle be squared?

I have no problem in killing someone who is about to murder innocent people to avenge Allah or whatever cause they believe in, but the consequences for those involved if a mistake is made are dire.

Which is what happened with the killing of Jean Charles de Menezes. The bombs of 7/7 had made London and its authorities nervous. On 22 July 2005, Commander Cressida Dick was 'Gold' as de Menezes travelled by bus to Stockwell

Tube station. She was in contact with two surveillance teams and a firearms squad comprising four officers.

Following the outrages on 7/7, when four suicide bombers had blasted three Tube trains and a double-decker bus, there had been failed attacks on 21 July – which the next day de Menezes was wrongly linked to.

The pressure was on everyone.

Yet that excuses no-one for seven bullets being pumped into the head of the innocent Jean Charles de Menezes. Such a catastrophe was bound to happen, but there was no need for the misinformation being trotted out by Commissioner Sir Ian Blair, a politically correct booby, not a proper bobby, more concerned about image than process.

The police were watching a flat where a suspected terrorist team were staying. A suspect came out of the house and one of the surveillance team was having a piss and missed him. Why was he the only one watching? Others must have been placed on all routes in case something like this happened. He was next seen on a bus.

He was followed and his movements must have been reported, and the surveillance team were concerned that he might have been carrying a bomb. He was heading for the Tube. Did he do this every morning or was this the first time? If this was his usual routine, what was so different with him on this day? If this was not his usual routine, then why was he not stopped on the bus or before he went into the Tube?

It was also said that he jumped the barrier; it seems that he bought a ticket and walked into the station. Why the delay in stopping him? If he was a real threat, a man with a big bomb, you'd get to him before he went down into the Tube system.

The order came from Gold, from Cressida Dick: 'Stop him!'

If you are following a suspect who you believe is going to kill innocent people, what does that mean to you? You are going to stop him so that he doesn't detonate that bomb. You kill him by shooting him in the head, not the body, for that's where the bomb is. You shoot him in the head and, fingers crossed, you've got the right man.

Why did it take so long for Commander Dick – promoted in 2006 after a glowing reference from Sir Ian Blair to deputy assistant commissioner and £130,000 a year – to issue her order? Surely, someone on the ground could have taken a decision earlier, and maybe avoided the death. If that was not the case, why let him go down into the Tube, where he could have killed so many people?

As Salman Rushdie said, we all live under a fatwa now. The UK laws must change to tackle head-on the terrorist threat and with it the procedures that the police have. The chain of command is too long. If a final decision has to be made it must be taken by a senior officer on the ground – not on the first floor of New Scotland Yard.

A catalogue of mistakes and poor lines of communication is to blame. A more streamlined process must be put in place, otherwise a killing like that of Jean Charles de Menezes will happen again. We must have officers who are ready to stand up and be counted, but they must be given support from the top.

There's too much concern with playing to an audience. Sir' Ian Blair did it, relying on the 'evidence' of confused witness reports he'd seen on Sky TV. His anti-terrorism chief, Andy Hayman, who was the assistant commissioner for specialist operations, also went to the microphones. The discussions about keeping people safe should be done behind closed doors and not for the benefit of the mass media. It seems especially risky to talk loudly when the full facts have not been established or verified.

I'd left the live-or-die pressures of Special Branch, but in Saudi Arabia it was only the climate and language that had changed. It was still a case of wearing a gun and protecting some of the world's top targets.

Chapter Seventeen
Chop Chop City

'The Devil can cite Scripture for his purpose.'
William Shakespeare, *The Merchant of Venice*

I'm now part of a largely unseen army that lives under the threat of death or kidnap every day. There are about forty-thousand of us employed by private military contractors (PMCs) and scattered throughout the Middle East.

In the early part of summer 2008 I had taken on a special assignment but, prior to that, I'd been working as a close-protection officer looking after European diplomats in Saudi Arabia. Some of the silent army work the bandit lands of Iraq and run an ongoing gauntlet of roadside bombs, suicide bombers, rocket-propelled grenades and machine-gun fire. They also get into frequent gunfights with insurgents.

These guys are mostly from the SAS and other Special Forces. The PMCs provide private protection and ferry around the engineers, developers, specialists and technicians.

The stories from Iraq are astonishing. Some of the roads are so dangerous as to be almost impassable. The route from

Baghdad to Amman, which passes Fallujah and Ramadi, is a shooting gallery and has seen many battles and deaths.

The British PMCs' style of operation is low-profile. They will bash up a car to make it look like an Iraqi runaround that's been damaged in a few shunts and they'll dress in Arab clothing and headgear. That's how they move the clients from one place to another. Some of the SAS guys on special jobs use tipper lorries or open-back trucks with a couple of goats tethered on to make them look like farmers going off to market.

Typically, when someone is being moved from one place to another, there will be a backup car, heavily armed with machine guns and high-calibre weapons, that shadows them. If the mini-convoy runs into trouble, the backup wagon stops and fights while the car carrying the principal takes off to safety.

It's not a Dogs of War operation. The PMCs are highly disciplined, corporate endeavours. British PMCs must be registered, pass a set of exams, and be regulated by the security industry authority, a government quango. They are also routinely hired through Foreign Office contacts to protect government staff who visit hazardous areas.

It's provided me with a unique opportunity to see the War on Terror from both sides of the divide. I have watched over the years the creeping radicalism of Islam, first with Salman Rushdie and the fatwa, and then 9/11. The stench of death has grown to unprecedented levels with no sign of abating; indeed, the opposite seems to be happening.

I find it hard to justify the decision by America and the UK to invade Iraq. This was taken in the pursuit of Osama bin Laden and al-Qaeda, and trying to find weapons of mass destruction, finally ending up with regime change in Iraq. I had no sympathy for Saddam Hussein or his murdering ways but to invade in the pursuit of WMD and removing him from power was a legal mess. Is the world a safer place because of these actions?

The genie has been let out of the bottle with no chance of getting it back in.

The First Gulf war in 1991 was justified when Iraq invaded Kuwait the year before. Blair and Bush's war against Iraq has been based on a perpetuating lie, which has put all of us in the front line. How can we defend ourselves against suicide bombers when all they want to do is die for the cause, and to sit with Allah?

In that climate I felt a little uncomfortable going to work in Saudi Arabia as a protection officer. And I hadn't even got the flavour of the place. Saudi Arabia is the home of what are considered the two most holy sites in Islam – Mecca and Medina – and cannot be visited by non-Muslims. It's also home to the most draconian and barbaric of penal systems.

In an area of Riyadh called Battah Market there is a square, known to Westerners as Chop Chop Square. Every Friday beheadings take place for major crimes such as murder and rape.

For small, everyday crimes such as theft, a hand is removed or fingernails ripped out. Westerners can get a ringside seat so that they will be deterred from committing such crimes. Most of the felons are from the itinerant workforce made up of Indian, Pakistani and Filipino workers. There is no such thing as a Saudi committing rape; if they are accused of rape then the woman is given fifty lashes for enticing the man.

It is a one-party state governed by the House of Saud. The

masterminds of al-Qaeda want to bring down the House of Saud, as they are allies of the West. Saudi is in the front line in the fight against terror. It is also one of the largest buyers of arms in the world.

Oh, and it produces more oil than any other country. Which is why the world's governments are hugely represented – and officials protected by guns for hire like me.

I have never seen a country where everything revolves around a religion. Mosques adorn every street corner and shopping centre. Prayers are called five times a day and everything stops for them at 5.00 a.m., and then at 12.30, 3.30, 6.00 and 7.30 p.m. All must attend. The Mattawan, the religious police – 'the prevention of vice and the promotion of virtue' – patrol the streets to enforce the call to prayer strictly.

Alcohol is forbidden, along with theatres and cinemas. To have a cup of coffee with your wife you must go to the family section in Starbucks and sit behind a curtain; this is the same for all places were men and women meet. Women are second-class citizens in every respect. On 12 May 2008 university professor Muhammad Ali Abu Razuza was caught in a coffee shop with a woman who was not a relative. No one has said what happened to the woman. The lecturer got 150 lashes and eight months in jail.

A lot of shops, instead of having music playing while you shop, play Koranic chanting. I went to my local garage to get my car repaired and the 'Allah Channel' was on. All religious festivals are practised, with the biggest being Ramadan, when the faithful are not allowed to eat from sunrise to sunset.

This strict way of life fuels radical fervour and therefore, if anyone transcends or offends Allah, retribution is sought. The Koran even states that if someone offends

Allah you can 'smite him down' and this has been going on since the Crusades.

The imams easily fuel the weak of mind to carry out the will of Allah. It has become such a problem for the Saudi government that they are planning to put CCTV in every mosque to combat the march of radicalism.

I saw Muslims rejoicing at the sight of the 7/7 attacks in London; they could see no wrong in these attacks. It is true that most of the people are outraged by these radicals. I met hospitable and friendly Muslims who welcomed me into their homes. But a short trip into one of the shanty towns, and it is a very different story. There's a madness, an evil, about them. They would stop at nothing. If they'd had even an inkling of what I did I would have been kidnapped and held for ransom. This is why people like me are housed in compounds surrounded by 12-foot-high walls and protected by the Saudi National Guard. It's like an open prison.

There is complete religious intolerance, and no one must insult the name of Allah or the prophet Mohammed. Muslims believe that Jesus was a prophet, the problem being that they think it blasphemous that Christians believe him to be the son of God.

They are starved of any other viewpoint, either religious or political. News is sanitised and heavily slanted; there is no such thing as balanced reporting. If a news article mentions Allah, then in parentheses after the name is 'peace be upon him' or 'PBUH'. At every opportunity praise and good wishes are heaped on the religion.

The tensions rose when I was in Saudi, and placed every Westerner in danger from the religious zealots. In 2005, a Danish newspaper, *Jyllands-Posten*, published some cartoons depicting Mohammed. Danish products such as butter were banned from the shelves. The only local difficulty was that, because of the bad Saudi diet, there is a very high rate of diabetes in the country. The Saudis import the bulk of their insulin from Denmark.

Stickers on the backs of vehicles were being displayed against Denmark and the West in general. Foreign embassies issued warnings of a backlash against us, advising people not to shop at busy times, to change travel routes and to vary times for going to and from work. The tension was palpable. For several weeks I was looked at with even greater suspicion and the locals would spit on the ground in front of me. With little else in the lives of the itinerant workers in places like Saudi, religion is the one thing they all have in common and can believe in. The imams can preach either peace or death, cherry-picking passages from the Koran to suit their purpose.

It was an intriguing experience working in Saudi Arabia and it has given me a view on Islam and some of its followers that is very unnerving, leaving me concerned for all our futures. I don't have to go to church every Sunday to be told to treat people with respect and to be a good person but every Friday a few imams preach hatred and death instead of peace.

I agree with the author Richard Dawkins, who said in his documentary, *The Root of All Evil?*, 'The time has come for people of reason to say enough is enough. Religious faith discourages independent thought, it's divisive and dangerous.'

In nearly thirty years as a policeman in the UK I have witnessed the always increasing appeasement of Islam for the sake of political expediency. When the borders of Europe opened, the UK under the Schengen Agreement maintained its border controls because of the IRA. We now face an even greater enemy and our borders must be strengthened.

Margaret Thatcher was asked many years ago by an Arab leader, 'When will we hear the call to prayer in your country?'

She replied, 'When we hear church bells in yours.'

Times have certainly changed.

And are changing. By the day.

Have Gun, Will Travel

'Many of these men have fought for
Queen and country and they're still putting their
lives in the firing line.'
Consulate official, Riyadh, Saudi Arabia, April 2008

The bomb exploded on the bus about 300 metres from my apartment. I was leaning over the balcony, sipping coffee and admiring the morning. I heard the screams of the injured. I ran downstairs and in my armoured car sped the other way to get to the Ambassador, my principal. If this was going to be a day of bombings, I needed to be close to the Ambo. His life was my responsibility.

The killings and bombings in 2008 were getting more frequent and closer to the centre of Colombo, and brought added pressure to the city and to those of us posted there to stop death. Sri Lanka was a country at war. No one spoke or wrote officially about it, but government hit squads were in operation and I was in the middle of it, protecting a senior foreign diplomat.

The politics are somewhat complex but the lethal line is that anyone or any organisation that upsets the status quo is extremely likely to be eliminated. The civil war has been raging for thirty years and with events as they are could easily turn into a one-hundred-year war; there is no sign of the horror stopping, with both sides claiming atrocities against each other.

Mano Ganetion is a Tamil MP and is a member of the Western Provincial People's Alliance. His party is affiliated to a larger party and speaks for Tamils. As a minority party in the Sri Lankan Parliament, they do not get much 'air time' other than raising Tamil issues and the war.

Yet Mano Ganetion constantly gets under the skin of the government on human-rights issues. The warfare wing of the People's Alliance are the Liberation Tigers of Tamil Eelam (LTTE), commonly known as the Tamil Tigers. They're what the IRA was to Sinn Féin, and Mano and his colleagues are not involved with the LTTE.

In late 2007 the Defence Secretary warned that the war would be escalated, as the LTTE had disregarded a ceasefire agreement. In turn, because of the increased military action, Tamil MPs became more vociferous in their condemnation of the government for its killing of civilians. In early 2007, a Tamil MP was assassinated by an unknown gunman, but it was clear that it was a government-sponsored killing, a brutal warning to others about overtly speaking out against the war.

The People's Alliance stepped up their verbal attack. The LTTE retaliated by placing bombs in Colombo.

With the breakdown of the ceasefire, daily terrorist attacks began, and not only in the capital but on softer targets around the country. At first it was military and government buildings that were seen as legitimate targets. It went quiet for what was only a moment, and the LTTE released a statement declaring that after the monsoon season they would increase their war actions. The rains passed and, true to their word, they placed bombs near military installations.

Towards the end of 2007, they changed tactics and blew up a shopping mall used mainly by Sri Lankans. Later that day a female suicide bomber blew up in a failed attempt to kill a Tamil MP who had turned against the LTTE.

I immediately increased security around the embassy and told the Ambo to cancel any meetings that could be rescheduled. The security around the embassy was increased. My government sources told me that if the situation deteriorated then the government would impose a curfew and close all schools. I briefed the staff on the current situation.

I suggested that they travel to and from work at different times and avoid shopping at peak times. I arranged for other means of transport for the local staff, so they need not travel by bus. Buses were becoming a big target for attack.

The daily outrages were starting to affect all aspects of life. The school run to the International School was now a concern. One of the main routes was along the Parliament Road, which was used by all government ministers when Parliament was sitting.

I was running out of options and men to cover all the security issues. Bombs were exploding constantly in the capital, and it would be only a matter of time before I was in the wrong place at the right time.

It got worse.

On 1 January 2008, another Tamil MP was killed. Again, it was state-sponsored, a revenge attack for an attempt to kill the head of the Sri Lankan Air Force. The LTTE missed the target but killed another minister instead. The two men had swapped cars and the junior minister had paid the price.

The civil war was getting really bad. The Defence Secretary went on television and said they would obliterate the LTTE by August. He announced a full-scale war. My heart sank. It's all very well killing people, but to go on national television and say you plan to wipe out hundreds and hundreds of civilians only fuelled the already bloody situation – and gave hope to the LTTE that, if they were not defeated by August, they could declare a partial victory.

All meetings out of the embassy were now a dangerous movement. Most of the meetings took place at the Ministry of Foreign Affairs. Security around government buildings was very tight, with many checkpoints.

It was a risk for me when we stopped at the checkpoints, because we had to open the door of our bulletproof vehicle. This shouldn't happen, but the intercom that allowed me to speak and hear the people outside the vehicle was defective. We had only the one armoured car and, because of the ongoing violence, we couldn't get it fixed. The other problem was the language. I had a local driver whom I trusted, but with so many guns around I was worried that some trigger-happy kid with a machine gun would blast off at the merest hint of a problem.

There were too many young kids with too many guns and just me in the middle.

The Ambo was getting more and more concerned for his safety as well as that of his family. I always tried to downplay the problem in order to reassure him that I was on top of the situation and had contingency plans for anything that might happen. In truth, I did not. I was in a foreign country with no means of any backup; I had to deal with it on my own and make those all important decisions instantly. The whole country was on alert and the days went by. If anything happened to his children or his wife, I had no plan to fall back on.

The Ambo was in his office and I was in mine, trying to get more information. I was trying to get information. It wasn't easy. They didn't trust me, or I them. I doubted some of the information that they were giving me and I tried to double-source it. My head was pounding. I was never very good at juggling but I was learning quickly.

With all this going on, I was called into the Ambo's office. He was sitting behind his desk looking at his computer. We were of similar ages and we had a good relationship, even though we had some toe-to-toe differences of opinion.

On the whole he was good to work with and, while his little knowledge of protection used to cause us friction, he respected my background. He stopped working and looked at me. I could see instantly that he was worried about something. I know the look.

Earlier in the morning a bus bomb had gone off, killing several people, including schoolchildren. The blood-spattered survivors ran screaming from the bus, away from the carnage of dead bodies ripped apart by the bomb only to be shot down by the terrorists, murdered as they ran.

It was not a good morning to be a parent. The Ambo said to me, 'My two children are on a school trip out of the city in two different locations. If something goes wrong I want to go and get them. Anyway, I'm thinking of going to get them now just in case something happens.'

I looked at him in utter disbelief. I couldn't help myself. 'You're fucking joking, aren't you?'

'I'm not. What's your plan?'

241

Plan? What plan? There was no plan. The plan would have been to keep them in the city, where I could get to them – and not on a school trip up the jungle!

I had to think on my feet and fast. This was not what I needed right now. Bombs were going off all over the country. Government and the military were the main targets and all of us at the embassy went to places where we were likely to be blown up.

Our local staff were getting worried and relied on me to advise them on the situation and now I was being told that the Ambo's children were out on a school trip at two different towns and he wanted to go and find them.

I told him that my plan was for him not to go gallivanting off into the country chasing shadows trying to find the children. There had been no immediate terror in the aftermath of that morning's bus bomb. If he wanted his children back we had to do it through their school, alert them and get them to take the kids to a safe hotel.

I told him I understood his concern but we would only put ourselves in danger as well as others by going out into the country. My plan was to stay put. Other ambassadors' children were on the same trip and, although concerned, they were happy to leave the school to deal with it. He wasn't overjoyed at my plan, but I kept eye contact to show to him that I was not going to back down. The whole emergency was volatile and fast-moving and could change at any time.

And it did. Another Tamil MP was killed courtesy of the government. The country was falling into anarchy with tit-for-tat killings. The Ambo received a phone call from Tamil MP Mano Ganetion. He was now in mortal fear for his life, believing he would be next to be murdered. The Ambo called me into his office.

'Mano's scared and wants to leave the country now. I said that I would help him. What do you think?'

'I think you're mad. If your name gets out to the government that you're helping Mano, then you'll be next in line to be killed. And, more than likely, that will mean me too. I strongly advise you, sir: don't get involved in this one.'

The Ambo has a strong spine. 'This is my job. He's a good and honest man. I'm going to help him whether you're with me or not.'

I couldn't believe what he was telling me. I was just about keeping a lid on Bomb City and he wanted to raise the stakes and put us all to the front of the firing line, top of the death squad hit list.

Now it was his turn to look me in the eye and see who would blink first. He had set his stall out and he was going to do it.

I said, 'OK, I'll help, but it will be done my way or no way. If you or the other guy don't do it my way then you're on your own.'

'I will do exactly as you ask and so will Mano.'

We went to a hotel and took the lift to the sixth floor. As we got out there were minders on the floor and along the corridor. One of these guys, after we had explained who we were, took us down the corridor and into one of the rooms. An impressive man about 5 foot 10 inches tall with thick, wavy hair stood up, came over to the Ambo and shook his hand warmly. He was visibly scared and very nervous.

The Ambo introduced me to Mano and he thanked me for my help. From the outset I said that he must do exactly as I said.

If he did, we would make it work; if not, we were all in trouble. The curtains in the room were open and I told one of his staff to close them. He looked at Mano and he nodded in agreement.

Where was he going to go? He first talked about Europe and the Ambo said that Norway and Holland were happy to have him. I pointed out visa restrictions. The Ambo looked at me and hurriedly made a few phone calls. He said the visa sections in both embassies would issue a visa within three hours.

Mano didn't seem to be impressed by this news. He said that he wanted to go to a country a little closer to home. At this time in his life, if he wanted have a life, he should be grateful for any kind of help.

I said, 'Let's do this another way. What flights are there tonight?'

One of his aides picked up his mobile phone and called a travel agent. There was a flight at 12.30 a.m. to India. Mano thought about it; for a man under a death threat he wasn't rushing along. Finally, he agreed to take the Air India flight. Both of them looked at me and asked, 'What do we do now?'

Since I was first dragged kicking and screaming into this nightmare scenario, I had been thinking of a plan. It wasn't much of a plan, but it was the only show in town.

'First, you must move out of the hotel. You're too well known to be here, and there are too many guests around. Any one of them could be your murderer. Find a safe house and stay there until I come to collect you. I also want the airport VIP suite booked. We're not standing with everyone else checking in and everyone looking at us.'

Calls were made and a house was found not far from the hotel. I asked for the address so that I could check it out.

'When I say it's safe, go to the house and stay there. I'll

come to the house at about 10 p.m. and wait with you until it's time to leave for the airport. We'll go in the armoured car and put you on the plane and wave you goodbye. I don't want all these men around me when we leave for the airport. It'll just be one car with you the Ambassador and me along with a driver. No one else. Is that clear?'

He nodded in agreement. I gave him my mobile-phone number and told him to call me if there were any problems. I took the Ambo back to the embassy and told him that I was going to check the house where he was going to wait. I took with me three of my team. I told them what was happening and they thought I was mad. I have to say that I agreed with them. It was an unusual situation but one that we had to manage. I gave them the address and we went to find the house.

It was in a main thoroughfare but set back off the street down its own driveway from the road. On each side was a high wall and growing over the wall were bushes. At the end of the drive were large, green, metal gates with a peephole in one of them so that any callers could be identified before being let in. The house and the drive were completely hidden from view until you got onto the main road. It was perfect.

I briefed my team that, if we were going to be hit, I didn't want them anywhere near me. I wanted this to be covert and give no outward signs of a VIP travelling in convoy. I wanted them to be a few hundred metres back from me. If they got caught at traffic lights, they were to stop and not jump them, to catch me up when they changed to green. If something did go wrong, they could come right in and give us help or take up firing positions from a safe distance. They agreed with the plan; I knew they would. It was the safest way.

We'd got use of an ambassador's vehicle, top-of-the-range

and a far higher-performance and safer car than the one we had. I spoke to the local driver. He seemed a good guy but there was no need to tell him too much at the moment. I just told him to pick me up from my embassy at 9.45 in the evening. I spun him a story: our official car had broken down and another ambassador had kindly lent us his vehicle. I then went back to the embassy and waited.

The government had informants everywhere and spies anywhere. The last thing we needed was for them to become aware of our collusion in helping an enemy of the state escape their clutches.

It was time to go and, when the driver got me to the safe house, I told him what the job was, just in case he wanted to pull out. To his credit he didn't. I then told him to go and get my Ambassador and bring him to the house. He left me on the pavement as he drove away.

I looked up and down the road, making a mental note of any cars and occupants close by. I then turned and walked down the driveway, where only the poor street lighting creeping through the trees hit the ground. I knocked on the gate and a small shutter opened and a head pressed itself to the opening. I told him who I was and the gates opened and he beckoned me into the courtyard. Two other vehicles were inside the grounds tucked away down the side of the house. I was invited in and sat down in one of the main rooms. It was a dark room with heavy mahogany furniture. It was very warm inside the house and no air conditioning was on. It was sweltering.

Mano came down the stairs, which were at the far end of the room. He sat with me, making polite but nervous conversation. I gave out an air of confidence but underneath

I was as anxious as he was. I was given a can of Coke, which I gratefully drank. The time passed slowly.

I called up my team and they were in place down the road waiting. The BMW reversed down the drive and through the gates, which were closed behind it. My Ambo was sitting in the car. I went out into the garden as the rear door opened and the Ambo was about to get out. I stopped him and said it was best for him to stay out of sight. Without speaking, he stayed in the car and closed the door.

Mano's staff put his cases into the car and we made our way down the drive and onto the road. I looked back down the road and saw our backup car pulling out from the kerb.

The roads were empty; if we were going to be hit then we'd spot the attack in good time. By now my driver knew whom we had in the car and he too was nervous, his hands gripping the steering wheel tight. I told him just to drive normally and try not to worry. The first set of lights were at red and he drove straight through them.

I leaned over and hissed in his ear, 'Don't do that! Drive normally. If that was normal, then do something abnormal and stop at the lights.'

The road to the airport was just that: one road; no other routes, no other roads, just this one. On either side of the road, about a block back on either side, was jungle. Over the course of the war a lot of assassinations have taken place on this road. It was a hot spot.

It was about 30 kilometres to the airport. The road was big but the main problem were buses. They run all night and they are frightening. The standard of driving is appalling. If two buses were together they would have a race to the next bus stop to collect the fare and make more money.

That was a minor worry. My biggest concern was that they were also a target to be blown up, and who was to say that they might not be used as a proxy bomb to take us out? We had no choice but to deal with the buses as normal. We couldn't avoid them. There were too many of them, and to do something out of the ordinary would attract attention.

We pulled into the airport road and approached the checkpoint. This was a formality, as we were in a diplomatic car. A cursory check of the occupants, and we were waved through to the VIP lounge checkpoint. Again, it was a simple check and the barrier opened and we went through. The three of us went into the VIP lounge and sat down. I sat some distance away so that I could get an all-round view of the suite.

The main doors opened and another VIP came in. It was a government minister. He stared at Mano and at my Ambo. The Ambo and Mano were talking and now everyone would now know what we had done. The game was up. The government minister was on his phone.

The flight was called and the three of us went to the gate. Mano thanked us again for our help and got on board. We waited for the doors to close, watched the wheels go up and left.

No one came to get us.

Driving back through the checkpoints, I said to the Ambo, 'I hope we don't become flavour of the month for the government and they decide to teach us a lesson.'

He didn't say a word. And nothing has happened.

Yet.

Glossary

AFO:	authorised firearms officer
AK-47:	Kalashnikov automatic rifle
al-Qaeda:	international terrorist network founded by Osama bin Laden (Arabic for 'the base' or 'the camp')
ambo:	informal term for ambassador
ASU:	active service unit (of the IRA)
DCI:	detective chief inspector
Del Boy:	Derek Trotter, a character in the British TV sitcom Only Fools and Horses, known for his dubious get-rich-quick schemes and wheeler-dealing
DI:	detective inspector
DPG:	Diplomatic Protection Group

dry cleaning:	term used by close-protection officers for checking that they are not being tailed while driving
DS:	detective sergeant
E4A:	special intelligence unit of the Royal Ulster Constabulary (RUC, now called the Police Service of Northern Ireland)
fatwa:	a ruling on a point of Islamic law; it could, and was in Salman Rushdie's case, be a call for someone's death
FCO:	Foreign and Commonwealth Office, British government department dedicated to promoting the interests of the UK abroad; usually called Foreign Office
G3:	a Heckler & Koch assault rifle
Gold:	designation of a police commander in charge of an operation
IRA:	Irish Republican Army
Kratos:	Operation Kratos, the code name used by the Met's SO13 (Anti-Terrorism Branch) to refer to policies concerning its shoot-to-kill tactics to be used in the case of terrorists or suicide bombers
MI5:	Security Service, or Military Intelligence, Section 5, the UK's counterintelligence and security agency

Glossary

MI6:	Secret Intelligence Service (SIS), or Military Intelligence, Section 6, the UK's external intelligence agency
MP5:	a Heckler & Koch submachine gun
M16:	a US 5.56mm military rifle
PIRA:	Provisional IRA (Irish Republican Army)
PMC:	private military contractor
Police Federation:	trade union for police ranks up to and including chief inspector
PPO:	personal protection officer
principal:	the person being protected by a close-protection team or officer
PSNI:	Police Service of Northern Ireland, formerly the Royal Ulster Constabulary (RUC)
SAS:	Special Air Services, an elite, specialist regiment of the British Army trained in commando techniques and clandestine operations
SB:	Special Branch (a unit of the police that deals with security matters)
SEG:	Special Escort Group, a team of armed police motorcyclists

SO19:   the Specialist Operations (SO)
         Firearm Command branch of the
         Metropolitan Police; still often
         referred to by its former designation
         of CO19 (Commissioner's Office 19)

Taser: proprietary term for an electric stun
         gun that immobilises a suspect/victim
         with electricity; first trialled in the
         UK in 2003

WFP: World Food Programme

WMD: weapons of mass destruction

XPD: extreme prejudice (Terminate with)